UPDATED THIRD EDITION

**GRAHAM WINTER**

FOREWORD BY **MARTIN BEAN CBE**

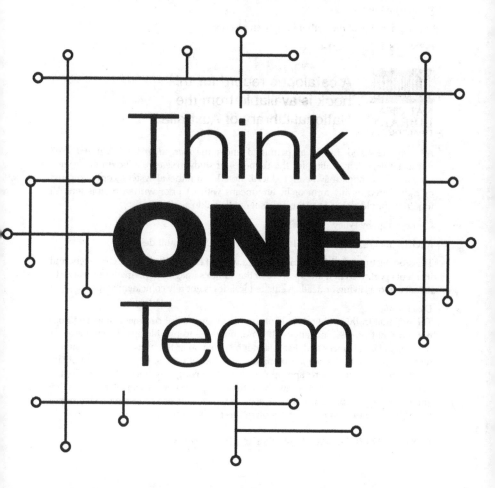

# Think **ONE** Team

The Essential Guide to
**Building and Connecting Teams**

WILEY

This third edition first published in 2024 by John Wiley & Sons Australia, Ltd
Level 4, 600 Bourke St, Melbourne Victoria 3000, Australia
First edition published in 2008
Second edition published in 2016

Typeset in 10.5/13 pt Palatino LT Std

© Graham Winter 2024

The moral rights of the author have been asserted

ISBN: 978-1-394-24104-0

**A catalogue record for this book is available from the National Library of Australia**

Cover design by Wiley

Internal images designed by Claire Magarey from Somersault design

The story featured in this book is entirely a work of fiction. The names, characters, and incidents portrayed in it are the work of the author's imagination. Any resemblance to actual persons, living or dead, events or localities is entirely coincidental.

**Disclaimer**
The material in this publication is of the nature of general comment only, and does not represent professional advice. It is not intended to provide specific guidance for particular circumstances and it should not be relied on as the basis for any decision to take action or not take action on any matter which it covers. Readers should obtain professional advice where appropriate, before making any such decision. To the maximum extent permitted by law, the author and publisher disclaim all responsibility and liability to any person, arising directly or indirectly from any person taking or not taking action based on the information in this publication.

SKY756C1379-B9FA-4A9E-9644-7E8E30FAF102_121823

*To Carol, Mark and Ben*

# contents

# about the author

Graham Winter is a best-selling author and adviser on leadership, teamwork and performance to leading Australian and international organisations.

He is the founder and Executive Director of Think One Team International and his background includes three-times Chief Psychologist to the Australian Olympic Team (including Sydney 2000) and six years as exclusive designer of High Performance Leadership programs for PwC Consulting in the Asia–Pacific.

As a Consultant and Performance Psychologist Graham has worked with thousands of leaders and teams across Australia and internationally.

His books include the bestseller *think one team, first be nimble* and his most recent book, *toolkit for turbulence,* which is becoming a must-read for leaders and professionals addressing the challenge to adapt and innovate in a volatile business world.

He is married with two sons and lives in Adelaide, from where he travels regularly to consult and advise clients.

Graham can be contacted through www.thinkoneteam.com.

# acknowledgements

Special thanks to my family, friends and colleagues who helped to bring *think one team* to life as a book and as a successful development and organisation change method for so many enterprises:

- Carol Winter for your love, support, pragmatism and willingness to always put yourself second to create the environment in which your boys have flourished.

- Kathy O'Donnell for your passion and attention to every detail that has made 'think one team' so successful. You even gave your name to a jelly-bean company!

- Kylie Smith for the countless things you have done to support me, our facilitators and all the clients who have embraced think one team. You always go beyond what is expected to make things better for everyone.

- Mark Winter for your challenging and innovative ideas, your commercial nous and for being a wonderful son.
- Martin Bean for being such a wonderful client, colleague, co-author of *toolkit for turbulence* and friend. Thank you for believing in me and contributing the foreword to this book.
- Ben Winter for the thousands of little ways you have supported me and brought joy to my life.
- Anne Carman for being a great colleague and source of common sense when it's needed most.
- Ron Steiner for your friendship, honest feedback, support and sense of humour.
- Gill Duck for your passion and commitment to developing leaders and teams to work as one.
- Mark Williams for being such a great facilitator and advocate for the think one team method and programs.
- Claire Magarey from Somersault Design for bringing our brand to life and being so delightfully patient when faced with our crazy ideas.
- Scott Eathorne for your great work in creating the publicity for think one team that keeps us front of mind in the business community.
- Nick Wallwork for seeing the potential in this book.
- Brett Penno for supporting us in the design and development of the think one team website.
- Frank Prez for professional advice and assistance over many years.
- The team at John Wiley & Sons Australia for your vision, guidance and support in bringing all of my books to the market.
- All our staff, facilitators, clients, partners and colleagues for your enthusiasm and willingness to make 'think one team' a way of doing business.

# foreword

In the ever-changing world of work, one thing remains constant: *great teamwork can make anything possible.* Throughout my career, I've seen the power of unity, collaboration, and shared goals to overcome enormous challenges and drive enterprises to greatness.

But I've also seen too many instances where disunity within and between teams had the opposite effect. It eroded trust, blocked collaboration, damaged performance, and left customers and stakeholders disappointed.

When I joined RMIT University as Vice Chancellor and President, an institution with over 80 000 students and more than 10 000 people, based in Melbourne Australia, with campuses in Vietnam and partnerships in Singapore and China, I was determined to make teamwork a trademark of my team and the whole university.

Given the size of our organisation I knew I needed more than just the conventional team building approach. Universities are large complex organisations and the structures and ways of working require a united leadership team and a one team ethos if your plan is to drive innovation and disruption and that's exactly what we intended to do.

Fortunately, I met Graham Winter and came to see firsthand the positive effect of the leadership and team tools and techniques he has so generously shared in this book.

We embraced the mindset and methods of Think One Team and made them our own. It began with my Executive Team sharing the big picture: committing to shared values and behaviours, aligning around a compelling vision, and adopting one team ways of working. As a team we grew from a collection of talented individuals who wanted to achieve great things to a team that knew how to align, collaborate and learn no matter what challenges came our way.

From there our broader leadership group embraced Think One Team tools to reimagine the way we formed, developed and sustained teams, bringing simple effective tools to make collaborative problem solving, partnering and small fast teams a key to our success.

If your aim is to create high-performing teams, capable of excelling in the dynamic and ever-changing world, then *think one team* is the book you must explore. Within its pages, you'll discover the essential context and tools required to become the coach your team truly requires. By doing so, you will not only unlock the potential to accomplish remarkable feats but also infuse your team with energy and satisfaction, much like my own team experienced as we navigated adversity and transformed it into a strategic advantage.

I currently have the great pleasure of advising and coaching CEOs throughout the world and I'm struck by how many of them don't take the time to build their leadership teams, they just assume it will happen because of the titles they carry. Sadly, those same CEOs are frustrated by hidden agendas, a lack of shared purpose, low levels of engagement and poorly thought through decisions. Don't take that path, read *think one team*, make it your own and apply the tools and techniques to unite your leaders, build a cohesive high performing team and create a one team culture that can make anything possible.

**Professor Martin Bean CBE**

# introduction

When the first edition of *think one team* posed the intriguing proposition, 'Imagine the possibilities when everyone in your organisation thinks and acts as one big team', both the publisher and author hoped this would spark interest among business leaders and teams.

History now tells us that the book, with its combination of engaging story and easy-to-implement model, created more than just a little attention and quickly became and remained a bestseller in Australia.

The first positive signals came from team leaders who bought the book because those three words—'think one team'—resonated as a solution to the silo mentality that causes so many of the frustrations of working in organisations of every size. I've lost count of the number of emails and conversations in which people have told me that the story could have been written about their organisation!

Those team leaders believed that their teams would enjoy and benefit from reading the story so they bought a copy for each person. This created a shared language and a way of opening up conversations about how they could work better together within and between teams. Many organisations in government and industry built on this by providing the book to all their employees to reinforce the work they were doing on organisational values, and leadership and team development.

As organisations became familiar with the 'think one team' method, many approached our consulting firm with requests for more tools and coaching to help leaders and teams to continue the journey of working as one instead of in silos. Our facilitators worked closely with many of these organisations across Australia and internationally and, not surprisingly, the methodology continued to evolve from experience and changes in business conditions.

Three specific developments have now all but transformed the way the 'think one team' method is implemented in organisations and it is those three changes that inspired this revised edition because clients regularly asked, 'Can we have a new edition that aligns with the methods and tools that we are now using in our business and with partners?'

The first and most significant of these developments is the business landscape of unstoppable, transformational change. Across all industries, the effects of digital technology, boundaryless competition and economic uncertainty continue to create an environment of almost limitless opportunity, enormous risk and massive challenge.

The main target audience for the book has always been the operations teams inside these organisations and they are, to paraphrase one of our clients, 'Working flat out to keep the lights on, while transforming into a new business model, and at the same time searching for a game-changing breakthrough before competitors find it'. It is these teams that have looked for guidance from change management and leadership development only to find that the former isn't designed for continual adaptive change, and the latter provides concepts but not a simple, practical toolkit.

It's because of these people that *think one team* has evolved to answer a bigger question than just, 'How do we fix the silo thinking?', from where it all began.

The new question is more fundamental, more crucial to the very survival of the business. It goes something like, 'How do we create a nimble and adaptive culture that equips us to thrive in these turbulent times?'

It seems so obvious now, but it took many an international assignment and the researching and writing of *first be nimble* to help our team realise that the answer was right in front of us.

While we focused on tools and practices that strengthened the collaboration within and between teams, we began applying an insight that came partially from performance psychology and partially from studying the way that adversaries came together to work as one team in a crisis.

In both settings we noticed that teams created a loop of conversations that we called 'Align–Collaborate–Learn' (ACL). For example, in a crisis, leaders create this fast loop of aligning goals and expectations, then going out in the field to work together and meeting again to debrief, and then repeating the cycle. Elite military, sports and first responder teams do the same and in all cases there is a timing or rhythm that suits the situation.

We encouraged teams and alliances to create this ACL loop using 'think one' tools such as team clipboards, collaborative problem solving and action debriefing.

They embraced it immediately because whether building a team, driving a change initiative or forming a new alliance it gave leaders a framework or scaffold from which to guide the development and ongoing performance.

As these ACL loops became more popular, we realised that we had stumbled inadvertently on a way to strengthen the one capability that's essential if a person, team or enterprise wants to adapt and even to shape their world. That capability is not vision, resilience, courage, communication, teamwork, alignment or any of a dozen other concepts. It is simply and powerfully the capability to learn together.

Peter Senge was right when he wrote, over thirty years ago, of the learning organisation[1]. By combining the 'think one team' tools with what we came to realise is a natural learning loop, we found that 'think one team' significantly enhances the ability of teams, colleagues, organisations and alliance partners to learn (and perform) together. The elimination of the silo effect is something of a bonus—because that dissipates when people are set up to learn together.

The second development is in collaborative technology, which accelerated dramatically in the early days of the COVID-19 pandemic. Driven by the initial imperative for connection, Zoom and Microsoft Teams have now become natural and essential tools for team communication, while ongoing development in cloud computing has spawned a vast array of collaboration platforms that support teamwork within and between teams.

The third development is the repositioning of 'think one team' as a solution to the frustrations that leaders express about the disconnect between linear, technical approaches to change management and a workplace where change is continual and disruptive.

As you will read throughout the book, we have ramped up the power and impact of 'think one team' by applying it in ninety-day cycles targeting real business change initiatives (within and across teams). Business unit leaders, project leaders and collaboration advocates use the tools and ACL framework to lead change through collaboration and co-creation. This is a far more nimble and adaptive approach than the highly planned conventional change management and delivers new capabilities and a business result at the same time.

And so, with these three developments in mind, my approach here is to preserve the spirit and style of the original book and in particular the story of The Big Jelly Bean Team where you will join the engaging, enlightening and at times funny transformation of O'Donnell's Jelly Bean Company from silo-afflicted to one team.

---

[1] Peter M Senge, *The Fifth Discipline*, Doubleday/Currency, 1990.

From its experiences you will learn the five practices that define the difference between 'think silos' and 'think one team', and see what these practices mean for leaders and employees across an organisation. All of this is presented in the context of developing the capabilities and culture that are essential to being a nimble, adaptive team or organisation.

From the vivid story, a 'think one team' method is built that you will find easy to understand and apply to your organisation. This method will give you a language to share across the business, and lots of ideas for thinking and acting as one team.

It's important to stress that 'think one team' is not a call to make your organisation one big department, because that will create the poison of bureaucracy. Rather, it's a simple yet powerful message for building the effective and enduring partnerships and collaboration that are needed among the people of your organisation to survive and thrive in a volatile business world.

'Think one team' is both a mantra and a philosophy of work because it offers a more productive and enjoyable way of living and working.

# O'Donnell's Jelly Bean Company organisational chart

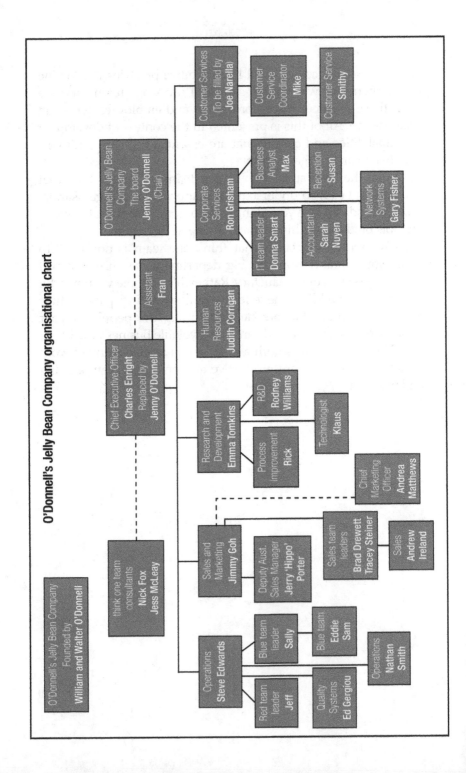

# part I

## the story of the big jelly bean team

Once upon a time, in a now-fashionable inner-city district of Sydney, Australia, a business called O'Donnell's Jelly Bean Company became the market leader in the confectionery industry.

Founded by brothers William and Walter O'Donnell on their return from the Second World War, O'Donnell's Jelly Bean Company was enormously proud of its seventy-year-plus history, its role as an employer of people from the local community and its profitability. Most of all, however, the people of O'Donnell's Jelly Bean Company were proud of its products.

It had been that way since William and Walter produced the first jelly beans in the kitchen of their home in Birchmore Street and sold them to children in the neighbouring streets. 'O'Donnell's', as the business came to be affectionately known, produced the best-looking, best-tasting and best-value jelly beans that money could buy. Any kid who lived near Birchmore Street could tell you that money spent on those monster-sized O'Donnell's jelly beans was a far superior investment to the bland fare at the local store, which carried all the 'brand' lollies. Importantly, an O'Donnell's jelly bean commanded a greater price when on-sold at school. Many children doubled their pocket money by investing in a few of those precious jelly beans and then selling them for a handsome profit at recess. The fame and profitability of William and Walter's jelly beans spread through the schools across the city and within a few months a small manufacturing plant was created at a site that has since grown to accommodate the nearly 500 employees of O'Donnell's Jelly Bean Company.

When you bought 'the real McCoy jelly bean' (as Walter loved to call it), you could choose from the three colours (red, blue and black) that O'Donnell's now manufactures in a gleaming, state-of-the-art factory. The enormous jelly beans (about the size of a bird's egg) were sold in clear cellophane packs of five, ten or fifteen containing the one colour of the customer's choice. The first jelly bean ever sold by William and Walter was red, so the teams on the red production line were suitably proud that not only did they produce the lowest cost jelly bean but also that theirs was the original 'real McCoy jelly bean'. The blue jelly bean has always been the most attractive, with its sky-blue coating and light-blue inside, giving it what the blue production teams called 'the sapphire look'. Last, but never least, was the black jelly bean, which, if you asked the black production teams, was the most popular choice of customers, the source of much media coverage and clearly a 'better jelly bean'.

O'Donnell's never sold a pack of jelly beans with the three colours combined.

Why? There were three simple reasons and they had all stood the test of time.

First, to sell them separately enticed customers to buy more than one pack, and the sales figures supported this view. Many a shopkeeper would tell the story of a mother and her children engaged in passionate debate over the need to buy 'a packet of each' so that the full range of O'Donnell's taste sensations could be enjoyed.

Second, William and Walter always believed that the unique flavours of the three beans would be lost if you put them together in a sealed packet.

Finally, there was no need to put those jelly beans together because year on year the company grew in revenue, profits and employees.

Until, as they have a habit of doing, things changed.

## g'day

They say that Sydney has the most beautiful harbour in the world and it sure looks like it from the left-side window seat as you fly into Kingsford Smith International Airport from the west. The Opera House and 'Coat Hanger' bridge are closer than I'd remembered, and more boats are now sprinkled across the sparkling bays and inlets.

As a part-time surfer I always think 'sharks' when I see that harbour. Did you know that more people have been attacked by sharks in Sydney Harbour than any other place in Australia? With nearly five million people living under our flight path I guess that's a lot of potential swimmers and shark bait.

Five years on the road is a long time. Last year I flew the equivalent of twenty times around the planet—mostly New York to London return, spiced up with increasingly frequent trips to Shanghai and Dubai. Leading a consulting outfit is exciting, but it's also high demand on everyone and everything.

My focus is big teams. Not those little departmental teams, but whole organisations and alliances: corporations, governments, universities, not-for-profits and even symphony orchestras. If they really want to unleash the phenomenal power that comes from being one big team, then my team can help to create the teamwork across boundaries that will make it happen.

Australia is home. Best place in the world to live. I'll be spending six months there writing a new book and creating tools and collaborative software in readiness to take on the greatest of challenges—disrupting the way enterprises across the world implement change.

I'm Nick Fox. I love jelly beans, Indian food, beaches and the awesome power of big teams.

This story is my way of sharing a few insights from the road about what might just happen to you and your organisation when everyone from the boss to the newest employee lives and breathes the mantra 'think one team'.

# real conversations

Tuesday, 8.58 am. The Executive Team of O'Donnell's Jelly Bean Company assembled for what promised to be anything but the usual 9 am executive meeting.

Walking to the boardroom from their plush offices, the team members crossed a foyer dominated (tastefully) by two identical displays of three two-metre-tall crystal cylinders on either side of the automatic glass entry doors. Each cylinder was full to the brim with those monster O'Donnell's jelly beans—red closest to the street, then black, then blue.

As you enter the O'Donnell's building, those jelly-bean cylinders escort you like a guard of honour towards Susan, the ever-smiling receptionist. An inconspicuous glass lid sits firmly atop each cylinder to ensure that no-one samples from the display. Floor lights project upwards to complete the striking effect.

By 9 am everyone was seated and attending to final emails on their phones and laptops. Cups of coffee and bottles of water sat on coasters to protect the lush, wood-grained table, the compulsory three dishes of jelly beans in the middle of the expansive table and papers at the ready.

Like most businesses, the O'Donnell's Executive Team was made up of the heads of each of the six key divisions:

- Operations (manufacturing and logistics)
- Sales and Marketing
- Research and Development
- Human Resources
- Corporate Services (finance, information systems and administration)
- Customer Services (currently without a division head).

The other member of the team, Charles Enright, was appointed Chief Executive fewer than three years ago after two decades with one of the world's leading strategy consulting firms. The position had become available due to the sudden death of the previous CEO, and Charles had convinced a former colleague turned headhunter to recommend him to the board, who were impressed by his CV, but—in hindsight—missed his glaring lack of people leadership skills.

A highly experienced consultant—who for some reason had cultivated an English accent without ever having lived in the country—Charles had a reputation for providing brutal feedback to company boards on the quality of their business strategies and leadership. He was rumoured to have confirmed more than once to his Saturday golf colleagues that 'O'Donnell's is extremely fortunate to have me'. No-one needed a rumour to confirm Charles's arrogance.

Since Charles had arrived, O'Donnell's executive meetings had been unpleasant and unproductive, with each leader giving an update on performance in their division followed almost automatically by a flurry of sharp, critical questions from the CEO.

'No excuses, no surprises, just results', was Charles's mantra, and it effectively smothered any strategic conversation and caused everyone to fall into line like compliant children.

Despite the CEO's uncompromising need for control, things started to unravel last year when the multinational Jellicoe Candy Corp parachuted into O'Donnell's most important markets, dropping O'Donnell's sales by more than 25 per cent in just six months. Now, twelve months later, the sales graphs were still heading south and only the cost savings from the first round of bitter redundancies temporarily halted the slide in profitability.

Everyone sat impassively as Charles opened the meeting in his typical threatening tone, with eyes fixed on the wall ahead of him, addressing the air in the room rather than his team members in person.

'Yesterday's board meeting was the most difficult in all of my time at O'Donnell's. The board is clearly of the view that the attempts to resolve the downslide of the past year have not been successful and unless this quarter's budget is achieved we will be compelled to cut 20 per cent of costs right across the company. I'm deeply insulted by the situation and have never in all my years in business seen a team that's worse at executing the business strategy.'

He paused to glare at the executives, one at a time.

'Find answers or heads will roll', he ordered while thumping the table for effect.

No-one spoke. For Steve Edwards, head of Operations and the newest (and most articulate) member of the team, it wasn't what he had expected on joining O'Donnell's six months ago, but the business challenge didn't particularly faze him. This was a good company—with good people and good products—that was ripe for growth.

What concerned him much more than the numbers was Charles's leadership style and its impact right through the business. Steve had seen executives 'burn the furniture' to make the figures look good. Invariably they killed the culture and the company in the process. Charles was a furniture burner if ever he'd seen one.

Steve would bide his time. There were things that could be done, and after three years in a bigger and more complex job in London he, more than anyone else in the room, saw huge opportunities in the challenges confronting O'Donnell's.

Never one to miss a chance to push his agenda, Ron Grisham, head of Corporate Services and self-appointed 'finance guru', took the opportunity while others were deep in thought to run through the numbers to support Charles, who he knew loved financial models.

'Our sales are down by more than 30 per cent quarter on quarter', he said, waving a complex-looking spreadsheet, 'and despite some minor productivity improvements in Operations I can't see an upside. My recommendation is that we make cuts now in Sales and Operations and don't wait until the April board meeting'.

Ron was pleased with how authoritative he sounded and looked to Charles for a nod of approval. It wasn't there.

Jimmy Goh, the dynamic head of Sales and Marketing, peered at Ron with a mixture of contempt and anger. This would be a poor choice of timing to tackle Ron's relentless pessimism, but Jimmy was almost angry enough to take him on anyway. Charles's clipped manner broke his thoughts.

'What's the real outlook on sales?' he asked, not even referring to Jimmy by name.

A Singaporean national with a Harvard MBA, Jimmy's energy and track record of success with confectionery companies in the United States and Asia earned him respect from all but Ron. As he replied to Charles's question, more than one member of the team was pondering why someone with Jimmy's CV would put up with this.

'The social media campaign has been revamped and is ready for launch early next month, and our multichannel partnering strategy is a potential game changer, so I anticipate a more than 20 per cent lift in revenue on the back of that in the US, Australia and Asia.'

He paused for a moment to gather his thoughts.

'The sales teams are up to the challenge, and if IT and Marketing get together and deliver on the channel partners' platform, I'm confident that we'll claw back what we've lost in market share and be ahead again within twelve months. It would be a mistake to overreact, particularly as the financial data we're getting is way out of date and our in-store and online customer numbers are already trending upwards.'

'With the greatest of respect', began Ron, running his hands through his thinning grey hair and bristling at the implication that his financial information was out of date, 'you haven't got within a mile of any of your sales forecasts for over a year, so why should we believe this one?'

Jimmy leaned forward and looked him squarely in the eyes. 'If you had any feel for the market instead of gazing out the back window and telling us where we've already been, you'd know that forecasting over the past twelve months has been impossible because the whole industry is being upended by cost pressures and new technology. The real numbers tell us that we're on the cusp of a breakthrough so only a fool would lose their nerve now.'

Ron was no match intellectually for Jimmy and certainly not in a verbal sparring match. He was fuming but knew enough not to take on Jimmy in this situation. He'd deal one-on-one with Charles and get those cuts in the Sales and Marketing budget that were long overdue.

Watching all of this unfold was Emma Tomkins, head of Research and Development, and the quietest member of the Executive Team. She joined O'Donnell's as a food technologist fresh from university and was appointed to her current role two years ago. Emma had been a superb number two in Research and Development, and very strong in project management and scientific rigour. A clever and insightful scientist, no-one but Emma was surprised when, at the age of thirty-two, she was appointed to an executive position, although to this day she preferred delving into an experiment to the cut and thrust of senior leadership conversations. Emma flicked documents across the screen on her laptop, hoping that someone else would break the silence.

'Charles, are you saying that the board has given us a quarter to turn this around?' enquired Judith Corrigan, Human Resources Executive. She wasn't going to let the meeting deteriorate into a slanging match and, like Steve, she'd seen plenty of situations worse than this during her career.

'Well, yes', he answered cautiously. 'The Chair and I expect a detailed plan to be presented at the next board meeting to address the financial situation. She has also asked me to meet her separately this morning, which I assume is to go over contingencies.'

Despite Charles's reputation for cutting down anyone who overstepped their authority or disagreed with him in public, Judith was determined to press forward. 'Okay, we seem to have two options: either we do as Ron suggests and start working on more reductions now or we back Jimmy to lift the sales performance.'

Not waiting for a reply, she turned to Steve. 'You've been an executive in a company that hit a massive hurdle and then picked itself up again. What do you think we should do?'

Steve was taken aback that Judith had tossed the ball to him. He'd only been in the job a few months and apart from the newness he was acutely aware that Charles seemed threatened by his experience and willingness to weigh in on matters of strategy.

All eyes focused on him, with everyone wondering whether he'd been tossed a ball or a hand grenade. It was a moment for leadership and Steve was both a natural and a well-developed leader.

He turned respectfully to Charles. 'Can I have a few minutes to work us through some ideas that I think are important?'

Charles couldn't refuse without looking defensive. 'Just a few minutes, we have a lot to cover', was his muted attempt at keeping the upstart Steve Edwards under control.

---

### real conversations

If you really want to know how a business is travelling don't go to the boardroom, go to the staff canteen.

People in boardrooms can lose connection with what actually makes the organisation tick. They miss the conversations, the emotional moments and the open tensions. Things are often controlled in boardrooms because of status and agendas. Steve knows that, but he's courageous and skilful enough to take the risk and bring a dose of harsh reality to Charles, Ron and his colleagues that they'll never get from a set of accountant's figures.

But first to the canteen, and to the conversations that tell us what's really happening at O'Donnell's.

---

# the staff canteen

Meanwhile, in the canteen staff milled around the coffee machines, while two eager players pounded a table tennis ball at each other in the far corner of the long, rectangular room.

Production had started at 6.30 am so Jeff (Red Team Leader), Sally (Blue Team Leader) and Customer Service Coordinator Mike were more than ready for coffee and a few minutes of downtime. They had joined O'Donnell's at about the same time five years ago and shared a common interest in tennis, which they played most Tuesday evenings in summer through the social club.

Mike and Jeff strolled halfway to the table tennis players and sat at one of the thirty or so round, laminated tables.

'How're things?' asked Sally, pulling up a chair and reaching for the sugar pourer.

Jeff put down his coffee mug. 'Pretty bad, actually. We're way down on production volume and everyone's scared that more redundancies are around the corner.'

'Yeah, same with us, although I hear that Sales is forecasting a big jump next month', Sally offered optimistically.

'That would be the same forecast they over-cooked last month', added Mike sarcastically. Sally and Jeff reluctantly nodded in agreement because they suspected that Mike was a sniper who enjoyed spreading targeted gossip, particularly if it was bad news. And they weren't about to be proven wrong by his next comment.

'I hear there's going to be blood on the floor at the exec meeting today. Davo from finance reckons that Ronnie Grisham's going to nail Jimmy about the forecasts and has you guys in his sights for some serious slash and burn.' He paused to smirk before adding, 'At least it would be good if something practical came out of an exec meeting instead of the secret club just keeping it all to themselves'.

Sally and Jeff could only agree with his last point. While their new boss, Steve Edwards, seemed to be making every attempt to keep them in the loop on what was happening, they had only a vague idea where the company was heading. Communication was just small-picture stuff and mostly negatives. 'Like putting a jigsaw together when there's no picture', Jeff had remarked at a recent meeting.

They sat quietly for a few moments. Sally's thoughts were on the mess-up with materials that she would have to fix when she went back to work. The Purchasing Department had decided that it could get a great price on red colouring, so without consulting with the production teams it had spent the entire monthly budget on red colouring. Now blue can't meet its targets for the week, while red is oversupplied and, as Jeff said, slowing down.

Mike didn't know it yet, but three of O'Donnell's customers, including the biggest specialist confectionery chain, were expecting the blue jelly beans for in-store promotions and would be on his case within twenty-four hours. Fortunately for Mike he would find a way to put the heat back on Sally and the IT Department even though he'd promised yesterday that everything was running to plan.

'Better get going', announced Jeff, standing and heading towards the dishwasher and passing two staff members who were furtively proof checking each other's résumés, which they would forward to local recruiters in the next week.

'See you', Sally and Mike replied together, before making their way back to work.

## current reality

Back at the executive meeting Steve stood and strode to the whiteboard on the far wall of the boardroom. Picking up a black marker pen he wrote 'Assumptions/old model' on the left and on the right-hand side he wrote 'Current reality'.

Turning to face the team, Steve began with an open question: 'What's the core idea that drives this business?'

Emma's scientific mind immediately wanted to clarify exactly what Steve was after.

'Do you mean, like Google aims to make the world's information accessible?'

'Exactly', replied Steve with an encouraging smile. 'The vast majority of successful businesses have a powerful core idea that pulls everything else into line. I'm interested to know if we are on one page about what that is for O'Donnell's.'

'We make a profit for shareholders', offered Ron, not quite understanding where this was heading but wanting to control it if he could. Judith grimaced but did her best to be constructive by adding, 'Quite right, and we do that by making the best jelly beans in the world'.

Steve smiled to himself as he scribbled Judith's words at the top of the writing screen and turned again to the team, who were mostly nodding in agreement. 'Are we absolutely and totally agreed on that?' he asked, pointing to the words:

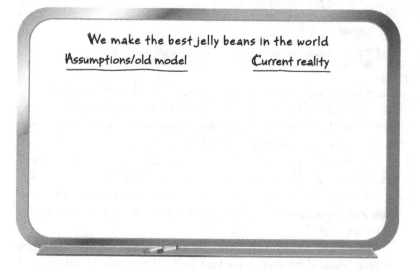

We make the best jelly beans in the world

Assumptions/old model            Current reality

Nods and grunts confirmed the driving force of the company for most of its seventy years. Steve continued, 'So, if that's the compelling idea that drives our business then what are the beliefs and assumptions about how to achieve that?'

After twenty minutes of increasingly lively discussion and some writing and rubbing out on the whiteboard (during which Charles did nothing but glare at Steve without blinking), a list of five points sat in the 'Old model' column:

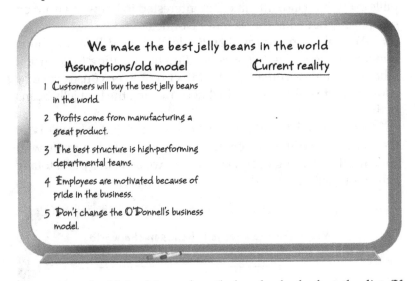

**We make the best jelly beans in the world**

| Assumptions/old model | Current reality |
|---|---|
| 1 Customers will buy the best jelly beans in the world. | |
| 2 Profits come from manufacturing a great product. | |
| 3 The best structure is high-performing departmental teams. | |
| 4 Employees are motivated because of pride in the business. | |
| 5 Don't change the O'Donnell's business model. | |

Steve scratched his chin and smiled as he looked at the list. 'If William and Walter were here today, I think they'd wholeheartedly agree that these are five compelling reasons why the business was so successful for many years. Do you agree?'

Everyone nodded, except Jimmy who had been uncharacteristically quiet since his run-in with Ron.

Steve pointed to the 'Old model' list. 'Unfortunately, like most business assumptions these were right for the past, but they are all wrong now.'

Charles's blood pressure jumped immediately, his mind yelling, 'How dare you think you can tell me what's wrong with this business!'

He remembered why he'd been so resentful when Jenny O'Donnell, the board Chair and daughter of William, had recommended Steve for the Operations job. 'Steve the upstart' had taken over the meeting and the team. This would stop as soon as Charles got him into his office on his own.

**open and honest**

O'Donnell's is a great example of a business that doesn't have open, honest and constructive debate at the senior management level.

Instead of tackling the tough issues, O'Donnell's has leaders like Charles, who use their status to aggressively stifle debate, and others like Emma, who avoid conflict at all costs.

Having the courage and skills to tackle the tough, constructive conversations is one of the first and most important steps in creating united leadership, which is the foundation on which big teams flourish.

Sensing an opportunity to ingratiate himself with Charles, Ron began to object, but Steve cut across him, determined not to let the moment be lost. 'Just a minute, Ron. Please let me finish and then we can fully debate it.'

Charles noticeably turned away as Steve started writing in the 'Current reality' column. Ron fumed, Emma wished the meeting would finish and Judith wondered just how this leadership team could ever be united enough to pull the company out of the looming crisis.

When Steve had finished, the whiteboard looked like this:

**We make the best jelly beans in the world**

| Assumptions/old model | Current reality |
|---|---|
| 1 Customers will buy the best jelly beans in the world. | 1 Customers are buying other products instead of ours. |
| 2 Profits come from manufacturing a great product. | 2 We are unprofitable. |
| 3 The best structure is high-performing departmental teams. | 3 Our divisions are underperforming silos that compete with each other. |
| 4 Employees are motivated because of pride in the business. | 4 Employees are disengaged and leaving. |
| 5 Don't change the O'Donnell's business model. | 5 Our business model is broken. |

Steve slid onto the chair at the end of the table and spoke quietly and sincerely to the team.

'I joined this business six months ago because I liked what I'd heard about the history of O'Donnell's and its amazing potential. In that time I haven't seen anything to suggest that we can't have a great future, but we have to create that future because the world has changed and we can't just let things keep drifting along as they are.

'There's no doubt that the last batch of redundancies and the other cuts were needed, and in my opinion, without those we would have slid even further. But it doesn't address the real reasons this company is in danger of failing completely.'

Charles bristled and glowed a deep red colour as Steve continued.

'There are two things that this company does not do and they are killing us.

'The first is teamwork. We aren't a team. From this Executive Team through every divisional team, we compete against each other for budgets, for resources and for recognition. We work in little teams with our own agendas and protect our own turf at all costs. Just go to a Sales and Operations meeting or a project review and you'll see that we don't really collaborate with each other—we just talk about it and then get busy again in our own silos.

'The second is change. We talk about being nimble and adaptive, but every day I hear people resist anything that even remotely upsets the familiar and comfortable routines. We just make our brilliant jelly beans and try to convince everyone that all is fine. But the reality is that people are not buying our jelly beans and we don't seem to get that.

'It seems to me that we have two paths. We can wither away slowly in our departmental silos or we can bite the bullet and work together to transform this business into a real competitor again.

'If we take the second path, I genuinely believe that we can become a greater company than William and Walter ever conceived, but it will demand united leadership from this Executive Team and a new culture of teamwork, collaboration and change readiness across O'Donnell's.'

Steve had said everything that he planned to say and then a whole lot more. Silence hung in the room as each executive took in the personal and business implications of a message that sounded like it had been delivered by a skilled CEO. They also feared how and when the narcissistic ex-strategy consultant turned Chief Executive would retaliate.

Charles's immediate need was to take back control, but he wouldn't be tackling Steve head on in the meeting. 'Thank you', he muttered, packing up his papers and bringing the meeting to a premature halt. 'I have a meeting with Jenny O'Donnell at 11 am so Steve let's meet at 1 pm in my office. We'll reconvene this executive meeting at 3 pm.'

Charles fully intended to have Steve's resignation to announce by that time.

Ron followed Charles out the door, while Judith congratulated Steve on his presentation. Emma and Jimmy left separately, each deep in thought about their own careers.

---

### be part of the problem

In the days before digital technology and economic crises disrupted the business world forever, it was common to hear people say, 'You need to be a part of the solution'.

The people of O'Donnell's no doubt want to be a part of the solution, but to deal with disruption and create some of their own, they must accept that they (with all the right intentions) are part of the problem.

Steve is prepared to put himself right in the middle of the problem and accept responsibility, while so-called leaders like Charles and Ron protect and defend the status quo and their own egos.

Disruption is no doubt hitting your organisation. If you want to take it on then first be prepared to acknowledge that you are part of the problem and then you'll be open to participate in all possible solutions.

---

## a resignation

Shortly after the meeting ended, Jimmy hesitated, then quietly knocked on the door before entering Charles's office. He had planned this moment for later in the week, but events were gaining momentum and he wasn't comfortable keeping the news from Charles while such important issues were on the table. He respected Charles for his analytical skills but found his ego overpowering. Not surprisingly Jimmy was much more concerned about bailing out on his team and colleagues than on the self-centred CEO who had rarely commanded loyalty from anyone in his business career.

Standing in front of Charles's desk, Jimmy was subdued but definite as he explained that he'd been approached by a headhunter and offered a job that was simply too good to refuse. He hadn't been looking outside, but sometimes things just happen. What Charles didn't know, and Jimmy couldn't tell him, was that two of his top account executives were almost certainly following him.

Charles slumped into the leather chair behind his desk. 'Where are you going?' he demanded.

Jimmy shook his head. 'I've signed a confidentiality agreement. I can't disclose it until I start there in six weeks' time.'

Charles shrugged, not really caring where Jimmy was going. If he'd known that it was Jellicoe Candy Corp there wasn't much he could have done, but he would have walked him straight out to the car park.

'I'll tell the Executive Team this afternoon', Charles announced sombrely.

'Sure, that's your call', replied Jimmy, feeling the urge to apologise but knowing that it didn't make sense to say you're sorry for something that you believed was the right thing to do.

## a new o'donnell

Jenny O'Donnell served five years on O'Donnell's board before succeeding her Uncle Walter as Chair on his passing twelve months ago. A lawyer and Chief Executive Officer of one of Sydney's better known legal practices, this was her first experience as a chair, although many years specialising in corporation law was an excellent grounding.

There were three principles that Jenny lived her life by:

- be clear about your intentions
- act decisively with courage
- give and earn respect.

They were what her father had drummed into her from her earliest years and they were written on a plaque that hung on her office wall. The three principles had helped William survive the war and build a successful business. For Jenny, they would guide her to rebuild and then transform what William and Walter had first created.

Charles had seen the plaque on Jenny O'Donnell's wall but taken no notice of it. Had he done that he might have better understood what she was about to tell him.

Jenny arrived at O'Donnell's a few minutes early and chatted briefly to Susan at reception before being ushered into the CEO's office. Their meetings were always slightly formal affairs. Charles didn't take easily to reporting to a person he believed had inherited the role, not earned it. Jenny, by contrast, gave and expected respect, which never seemed easy with Charles.

Jenny got straight to the point. 'The board held an extraordinary meeting last evening to discuss the company's situation.'

Charles was stunned that the board had met without him. 'We haven't taken this decision lightly, but we have made the decision to seek your immediate resignation.'

Jenny waited for a reaction. Charles went bright red and was soon gasping for breath.

Charles would recover from the panic attack, although being carried by ambulance stretcher across the foyer watched by startled employees wasn't what he or Jenny would have wanted. That was perhaps the only thing on which they agreed, thought Jenny, as she sat quietly in the now-vacant Chief Executive's office and pondered the next steps in her plan to transform O'Donnell's Jelly Bean Company.

# get the values off the wall

O'Donnell's was abuzz with rumours, mostly exaggerated but all tinged with an excitement that maybe—just maybe—the company would be rid of the arrogant control freak Charles Enright.

Production teams milled around eager to hear the latest bulletin on Charles's condition. Sales staff scanned social media for the juiciest gossip and even the studious finance team huddled together sharing a joke at the Chief Executive's expense.

Certainly not many people were upset by Charles's horizontal departure through the foyer, and the words 'Total Eclipse!' scrawled across the whiteboard in the sales meeting room captured the mood of many who were of the view that Charles sincerely believed the sun rose from his own backside.

Depending on where you walked around the company, Charles had variously died from a heart attack, been paralysed by a stroke, choked on a ham sandwich or been punched out by Jenny O'Donnell, although the last theory was more wishful thinking than believable.

No-one knew or even expected that Charles had been sacked or that an O'Donnell was again about to lead the business. There were plenty of surprises coming and even a few that would catch Jenny O'Donnell unawares.

## a transformation

Jenny O'Donnell sat at the CEO's desk as her father had years before, knowing that the future of the business rested in her hands.

Reaching for her phone, she punched in a local number and waited.

A relaxed Australian accent tinged slightly with an American twang answered almost instantly.'Morning, Nick Fox speaking.'

'Nick, Jenny O'Donnell here', was the more serious reply.

'Hi, Jenny, nice to hear from you. How's Sydney's brightest and best legal mind this sunny morning?'

'Nick, I'm fine, but it's not a legal matter that I'm calling you about.'

When something was particularly serious Jenny had a habit of beginning her sentences with a person's name and Nick knew her well enough to spot this and shift to business mode.

He listened intently while Jenny rattled off a brisk yet detailed account of O'Donnell's recent history. It was the brief you would expect from a good lawyer: succinct, structured, punctuated with facts to support the main themes and culminating in a summary of the key points and actions.

'The grapevine tells me that you're not back in Australia looking for work, Nick, so I can fully understand if this is just a catch-up call and we head off in separate directions.'

She paused, while Nick waited and wondered what Jenny had in mind.

'I really need some help to turn this business around. The fundamentals are all there and I'm sure it wouldn't surprise you that the current problems are more to do with culture than numbers. Nick, this is a great team waiting to be unleashed, and that's your bread and butter.'

Nick's plans for the next six months were to write a new book and find a breakthrough idea for his own business. Getting involved in a jelly-bean company in Sydney wasn't exactly in his frame, but something about this appealed.

Besides, Nick liked Jenny and had huge respect for her integrity and the O'Donnell's business. He decided he would help her if he could.

'What if I jump in a cab and we at least catch up for a coffee to chat through the issues?'

'That would be great', she replied warmly. 'Can you be here around 1 pm?'

'Sure can. I'll see you then.'

From the beach-side apartment that he had rented for a week to catch a few waves and do some business, it was only a short drive to O'Donnell's. Nick knew the layout from many years ago when he'd interviewed Jenny's father while doing some of his initial research work on big teams, before heading off to the United States.

As he sat in the taxi reflecting on how much the business world had transformed in recent years, the new Chief Executive was already notifying the Executive Team to meet in the boardroom at 3 pm. If things went well, it would be their first introduction to Nick Fox and her intention to transform O'Donnell's from its many and varied silos into one big, formidable team.

A few minutes later Nick was walking between cylinders of blue, red and black jelly beans that ushered him towards the still-smiling Susan.

---

**you're only a new boss once**

When I took over one of the first teams in my business career someone advised me that 'you're only a new boss once'. Unfortunately, there's a difference between being told something and actually listening!

---

*(continued)*

---

**you're only a new boss once *(cont'd)***

Six months into the job I realised that I hadn't had the conversations with my team that clearly defined a game plan everyone bought into. The misunderstandings and conflicts showed a serious lack of leadership on my part. I'd missed the chance to shape the important things, to create a compelling big picture while still new, and as the newness wore off it seemed ten times more difficult to get people engaged.

Jenny has that window of opportunity to create new expectations and standards for O'Donnell's. If she hasn't had an impact within six months, she'll also learn the hard way that you're only a new boss once.

---

# 1 pm, coogee beach, sydney

Sam and Eddie sat outside the breaking waves hoping for one last ride to finish what had been a great surf session. The offshore breeze had stayed soft but steady all morning and there was no hint that a sea breeze would ruffle the still-solid one-metre swell that was barrelling over the sandbars.

'What do you reckon?' asked Eddie, the evening-shift Maintenance Team Leader for O'Donnell's blue team.

Sam, a technician on the blue team, was much more interested in extra surf time than the evening shift at O'Donnell's. 'Let's just paddle in and call in sick', he replied.

'You can't just call from the beach—the seagulls will give it away', laughed Eddie, spinning his board and stroking hard as a larger swell started to lift 50 metres seawards. 'See you on the beach.'

They both caught the same wave, with Eddie, the more senior at work and on a wave, getting the clear water, while Sam got crunched as the wave ledged on the shallow inner sandbar. Shaking the sand from a shaggy mop of jet black hair, Sam jogged, board under his arm, to join his colleague at the small pile of clothes and towels on the dry sand.

'You know, I'd never have done this three years ago', said Eddie to the slightly distracted Sam who was watching a lifeguard, rescue-board in tow, dashing towards a swimmer who was flailing helplessly in the rip. 'Yeah', grunted Sam, 'but it was an awesome place to work then because everyone got on'.

'That mongrel Enright stuffed it up', mused Eddie to himself as Sam attempted to towel dry his unruly hair.

'I say we go up behind the Coogee Hotel, find a quiet spot and each call HR', suggested Sam. 'You can have food poisoning and I'll have a migraine.'

'Bloody hell!' exclaimed Eddie, staring at the text message on his mobile phone from one of the day-shift maintenance guys. It read, 'Enright's dead or something. Chaos here. Suggest you stay at beach. See you at Coogee pub at 7'.

Twenty minutes later they'd both called to advise of their sudden illnesses and were re-waxing their boards in anticipation of another few hours in the now-rising swell.

'They don't treat us like we're part of a team, so I reckon we deserve a day off occasionally', yelled Sam as he ran at the shore break, skilfully jumped feet-first onto his board and slid up over the crashing wave. Eddie wasn't quite as cynical as Sam, but like a growing number of O'Donnell's staff, sick leave was a way to bring some fun back into what had become a daily grind. And no-one wins when people lose their passion for a company.

He paddled out along the rip line, dodging a couple of surfers flicking off at the end of their rides, and leaving it to others at O'Donnell's to scramble through the evening shift without their usual maintenance cover.

## never leave a vacuum

Over the years, Nick Fox and his team had devised a short, sharp set of core principles for guiding leaders as they set about building and connecting their teams. One of those principles, 'never leave a vacuum', is a reminder to be vigilant in preventing any communication gaps between management and key stakeholders such as staff, business partners and owners. When things are uncertain or changing, people soon create their own (usually false) rumours if that communication is missing.

Nick had heard himself countless times encouraging leaders to 'never leave a vacuum'. It was a double-edged principle for leaders: 'Send crystal clear messages, while keeping the organisation agile and ready to adapt and change in an instant'.

Charles Enright would have dismissed the expression 'change in an instant' as evidence of poor strategy and execution, but Jenny O'Donnell knew what it meant and why it was so important to a company facing waves of disruption from competitors, technology and the economy.

Within thirty minutes, Jenny and Nick had crafted a brief note to all staff advising that Charles's health was fine and that there would be an all-staff meeting addressed by Jenny at 4 pm the next day in the canteen (coinciding with shift change).

Most of the staff knew Jenny through the regular plant visits that she had insisted on, despite Charles's irritation at having the board chair strolling through *his* business. Her pleasant and engaging manner had seemed such a contrast to the Chief Executive's cold, uncaring style and, of course, some of the longer serving staff knew her as a child, so there was a natural affection for her and a connection to a time when O'Donnell's was like one big family.

This was now a family that needed some 'tough love' but one thing could be assured—there would be no leadership vacuum while Jenny O'Donnell was in charge.

## when strengths become weaknesses

'Nick, would you be willing to attend the executive meeting at 3 pm?' Jenny paused and waited for his reaction and then continued when he agreed. 'There are so many things that this business has done wrongly over the past three years and one of the most important is that we've destroyed a lot of the good things about the culture without replacing them with a better option.'

She filled in a few more gaps including how, unbeknown to Charles, a subcommittee of the board had spoken privately with three members of the Executive Team (Judith from HR, Steve from Operations and Jimmy from Sales and Marketing) and with the best intentions for the business each had been willing to share their views on the current reality of the business.

Jenny preferred not to go behind the CEO's back; however, she and other board members had suspected that Charles was using his ample intellect to produce spectacularly impressive reports to put a positive spin on a deteriorating situation. The discussions had only heightened her concerns, leading to her urgent recommendation—which was accepted by the board last evening—to fire Charles and replace him with Jenny.

Nick listened intently to Jenny's briefing, interrupting just once to ask, 'I'm assuming that many of the strengths of the company's culture have become weaknesses as the market has changed in the past few years?'

'Absolutely', she replied. 'We've always valued family-style stability and friendliness, which was great when things were changing slowly, but now the market is so volatile we need to be constantly challenging and changing. People just don't know how to do that because they think a robust conversation is a sign of disrespect and there are plenty of staff complaining about change fatigue when we haven't actually changed anything significant!'

Nick laughed at the familiarity of the story. It was the same across many organisations where strengths of culture that had built global companies over decades had become weaknesses overnight as the organisations scrambled to confront the way new technologies changed business models and introduced new competitors.

'It's hard to give up on what's made you successful in the past, but if we don't disrupt our own businesses someone else will do it for us', Nick observed, thinking as much about his own organisation as about O'Donnell's.

# 3 pm executive meeting — end of the spin

The Executive Team sat motionless while Jenny briefly introduced Nick as a consultant with a role that she would explain later.

Nick sat back from the table while Jenny confirmed that Charles's condition was not serious, and then immediately hit them with the bombshell that the little loved or respected CEO had been asked by the board to resign. She stressed that her first step in getting more honesty and openness into the business was to confront reality and not put a spin on it—Charles had led the business poorly and that couldn't continue.

Had the team been fitted with heart-rate monitors, it would have been Ron Grisham's heart that was pounding the fastest as he feared he might be next in the board's sights.

Jenny continued, aware that no-one in the room wanted to discuss anything as yet.

'The board has asked me to take the role of CEO, commencing immediately.'

Two executive panic attacks in a day would have been unlikely, but Ron's reaction was as close as you get while trying to sit impassively at a board table with your career flashing before your eyes. Nick thought Ron's complexion matched the red jelly beans.

'There are three immediate pieces of business to address, so let's cut straight to the issues.

'First, I want everyone to be totally clear about what I see as the future for O'Donnell's.

'Second, there are critical short-term business problems with cash flow and customers that must be resolved.

'Third, I want to fully introduce Nick Fox, who will play an important role in helping us to work together as an effective leadership team.

'After that I will meet with each of you individually in my office, starting immediately after this meeting, to agree on what we expect of each other and to discuss your role in taking this business forward.'

### credible, concise and, above all, compelling

Jenny was about to lead a transformation of O'Donnell's that would upset power bases, abolish entrenched practices and forever alter the day-to-day work of many people.

Despite the obvious challenges faced by the company, it would be a difficult task getting everyone on board because people do not easily embrace this level of change. In reality we all consciously or subconsciously know that there are three choices available when we get a strong message to change: the first is to embrace the change; the second is to resist (passively or actively); and the third is to walk away.

To be an effective leader of change, you should give people two choices, not three.

In other words, you need to communicate both the imperative to change and the reality that staying with the status quo is not an option. This isn't a threat—it's a statement of reality that forces the choice to either go with the change or leave.

To inspire people to join you in shaping the future, apply these three standards to the story you tell them:

▶ *be credible*—your story must make logical sense to all your stakeholders, from employees to investors

▶ *be concise*—ensure your story conveys the message with minimal words or images

▶ *be compelling*—your story must be emotionally compelling to your audience.

Too many leaders make it logical and concise but fail to create the emotional case to challenge and change the status quo. Sometimes that's about inspiring words and actions, and sometimes it's about burning a few bridges so people can't go back to the comfort of the past.

Jenny intended to do both.

Over the next thirty minutes Jenny told the story of how William and Walter created O'Donnell's Jelly Bean Company, and of the values that underpinned the business. She spoke of passion, of their first foray into large jelly beans and the creation of a 'cook, pack and ship' production line that revolutionised the industry and brought respect from competitors and colleagues alike. She described their fanatical concern for creating a product that consistently delighted their customers. And finally, she spoke of the pride that William and Walter felt as people approached them seeking to work at O'Donnell's because of the strong team bond, the supportive management and the enjoyable workplace.

Her voice was tinged with a fierce resolve as she told how O'Donnell's had lost its way.

'Instead of setting the pace in our industry, we've created a boring "me too" business that any MBA student could reproduce in a week.

'Instead of delighting customers, we've disappeared from their view because new competitors and channels have more aggressively targeted them.

And instead of teamwork, we're making an art form out of competing against ourselves for budgets, time, resources and people. Any sense of passion and fun seems to have been squeezed out of the place.'

'Look at the wall', she said, pointing at a rather jaded-looking poster with the words 'Delighted Customers', 'Passionate Team' and 'Respected Business'.

'Our values are on the wall but they don't mean a thing. I've spoken privately to quite a few staff over recent months and, quite frankly, they think the values are a joke.

'So, starting from this moment we will return to our roots to build a new future. We will refresh those values, but the essence of each one will remain at the core of what we do.

'As the leaders of O'Donnell's, we are all accountable every moment of the day to put those values back into the heart of this company.

'I expect you all, and myself, to live, breathe and be the values 24/7. They must become our trademark as a united leadership team.'

She paused for effect, then turned towards the visitor. 'And that is why I've asked Nick Fox to join us today.'

---

**values 24/7**

You've probably got values posters on the wall in your organisation, but do the values genuinely mean something to you and the people you work with on a day-to-day basis?

Core values are absolutely essential for creating a flexible, high-performing organisation. Whereas in the past managers relied on rules and regulations, the best change leaders trust people to use the values to guide their decisions when they're under pressure. This empowers people and helps everyone to move quickly to adapt to change.

The journey for O'Donnell's, and perhaps for your business, is to instil into people specific and meaningful values that they can live by 24/7 so that they don't switch them on and off when they walk through their work door every day.

---

Jenny was impressive and Nick couldn't help but be caught up in the energy of her ideas and determination as she began her detailed introduction of him.

'Nick and his team specialise in helping organisations to create a nimble, team-based culture. Steve, I think you know Nick from work that he did with you in London?'

Steve nodded. He was a fan of the simple, one-team method and tools because they engaged everyone from executive to front line. It was also a welcome relief from the usual menu of leadership workshops and complicated change management plans.

Jenny continued, 'Nick, we've got a great company. But we've lost our way and need to change really quickly to get back in the game. I know that you and your team have lots of things happening, but we'd really appreciate your help'.

All eyes turned to their guest. Steve caught his eye and shrugged. Nick knew he was hooked.

'Sure', he replied immediately, 'it sounds like fun'.

# divided we fall

A week earlier, Jenny O' Donnell had sat alone in the Qantas lounge at Sydney airport waiting for a delayed flight to Melbourne.

Two O'Donnell's Sales Team Leaders, Brad Drewett and Tracey Steiner, were sitting in nearby lounge chairs and Jenny couldn't help but overhear their conversation. Tracey was upset about something at work, and Brad was agreeing with her.

'Sales seems to get the blame for everything in this place and yet just look at how other people screw up.' Brad nodded as she went on. 'If IT had their act together we could actually be prepared when we get in front of clients instead of them knowing more about O'Donnell's than we do. I mean, how embarrassing was it last week in Singapore when I was told by the client that we were two weeks behind on delivery? You can imagine the chances of hitting budget on that account.'

'Couldn't agree more', added Brad. He continued, 'And what about R&D? Do you think there's any chance they could get within 10 kilometres of a real customer before telling the world about their next wonder product?'

'No more likely than Marketing sharing the promotional campaign with us before we start getting calls from clients about discounts that some genius in head office has promised them', replied Tracey.

There was a tension in her voice that sounded a lot more serious than a gripe session among colleagues. 'Which is why I'm out of here as soon as another job comes along.'

Brad laughed. 'Yeah, that's assuming that HR can process your resignation in time!'

Jenny cringed. She was sure that O'Donnell's wasn't as bad as the conversation suggested, but these were two of the brightest stars in the talent pool list that went to the board last month, so if talent was unhappy enough to walk out the door, then there were big problems that had to be addressed.

---

### no spectators

Did you notice how Brad and Tracey have become negative spectators in their own company?

Spectators are dangerous because they see themselves as above the game and either can't or won't take responsibility for fixing things. They only see problems instead of opportunities; they fortify the walls between departments and levels of hierarchy; and worse still, they suck the energy out of the people who really want to give it a go.

The best way to engage the spectators is to involve them in co-creating solutions to problems and opportunities. This is why our first activity in 'toxic cultures' is to implement a collaborative problem-solving initiative. We give people ninety days. They get no opportunity to sit on the outside. They are in the tent, learning and using one-team tools with their colleagues. You find out pretty quickly who wants to play and who prefers to just watch!

Pause and reflect for a moment: how many people in your team or organisation are more 'spectator' than 'player'? Which are you? When does the ninety days begin?

---

## setting the highest bar

Jenny, Nick and the Executive Team gave themselves less than twenty-four hours to prepare for a presentation to all staff, so every minute was vital.

Nick headed off with Judith to get the quick-fire briefing on the business that he needed before running an introduction to the think one team method for the Executive Team in the morning.

Not surprisingly, Jenny was fully prepared for the one-on-one meetings with the executives and first up was Ron Grisham. That was Jenny's choice. As was the agenda.

Forever the 'control freak', Ron immediately offered to go over the finances but Jenny quickly made it clear that she knew enough about that for the moment. 'I don't intend to discuss the numbers, Ron. My interest today is how you and I might work together in the future.'

Taking advantage of Charles's narcissism had been a perfect way for Ron to hide his bullying. He enjoyed doing Charles's bidding knowing that threatening to drag a fearful staff member into the Chief Executive's office was the quickest way to get what you wanted. Ron didn't see himself as a bully, but Jenny did and that sort of behaviour would never be accepted in a business that she led.

In fifteen business-like minutes, Jenny outlined her expectations, described the behaviour she did and did not expect of individual executives and clearly, almost surgically, described the toxic effects of Ron's behaviour on the culture of the business. Finishing on a more constructive note, she acknowledged his financial skills and offered to support him in developing his people skills. But there was a caveat—it had to be fast-track improvement or she would replace him. No second chances. Ron left shell-shocked and with much to consider.

One by one each executive received the same clear, unequivocal message: executive leadership means accountability to deliver exceptional results and to live the values in every action and conversation. There was no direct threat in what Jenny had said. It was a statement of fact that left no doubt that she intended to set the highest bar on everything for herself and the team.

---

**show you care: go one-on-one**

Leaders lift the attitudes, emotions and behaviours of other people, but they don't all do it the same way.

Few people have the charisma and substance to inspire from the soapbox; however, even the quietest of leaders can be incredibly powerful in one-on-one conversation.

---

> As a general rule (whether you are CEO or a first-time team leader), the more time you spend one-on-one with your team (without micro-managing), the more success you'll have as a leader. Why? Because it shows you care about the person and it sets them up to succeed.

The final one-on-one meeting late in the evening was with Jimmy Goh, the Sales and Marketing Manager who had resigned almost twelve hours earlier to a person who was carried out on a stretcher and no longer worked in the business.

'Jimmy, I know that you are leaving us and I am very disappointed.'

'Charles told you?' Jimmy asked in surprise.

'No, your future employer isn't very good at keeping a secret.'

Jimmy was at a loss for words.

'The board understands your frustration with Charles. In fact, your impending departure was one of the final straws that broke the camel's back last night and led to the decision.'

O'Donnell's desperately needed Jimmy's capabilities, energy and experience. Jenny certainly didn't want him playing for the opposition, and so she was resolute about finding any way to get him to go back on the offer from Jellicoe Candy Corp. It was close to midnight when he agreed to give it more thought and then to have a further discussion after the staff meeting. Jenny hoped that the session with Nick in the morning and the full staff meeting in the afternoon might just build enough momentum to push her Sales and Marketing Manager to give it a second go.

Jimmy was more than a little uneasy that the confidentiality on his new job had been broken by his future employer. Maybe with Jenny in charge it might be a better option to stay, but he was too tired to make a career decision at that time of night.

# chapter 3
# the compelling case

It was a weary Executive Team that gathered in the larger of the two O'Donnell's training rooms at 9 am on Wednesday to hear what Nick Fox had to say. Joining them were ten managers and team leaders from across the business who had been personally asked by Jenny to attend and openly participate.

Their attendance, and subsequent role as collaboration advocates, was just one of many steps that she would take to unlock the 'executive club' and to make one-team collaboration the centrepiece for driving transformational change across the whole of O'Donnell's.

'Morning, everyone', Nick began with his customary openness.

There was barely a flicker from the group and he knew that their minds were elsewhere, focused on the unfolding turmoil in the business.

'Have you ever heard of the Three Kingdoms?'

It was a hook, intended to capture their attention, and it worked immediately. Jimmy responded, 'It's a part of Chinese history'.

'It is', replied Nick, 'and it's repeating itself in O'Donnell's and in most twenty-first-century organisations'.

Now he had everyone's attention, but only for as long as he promised to be part of the solution and not a distraction.

'Let me briefly explain.'

Nick flicked a slide onto the projection screen showing a typical Chinese scene and recounted the story of the period in Chinese history following the Han Dynasty (a period of stability and unification) when the great country was divided into three smaller kingdoms, each of which developed its own laws and ways of life.

A good storyteller, he had everyone's attention as he described how for 300 years from approximately AD 220, China's Three Kingdoms fought each other, and even though there were periods in that time when China was unified, it quickly fell apart again. He highlighted that this tension created many good things, such as beautiful art and strong local communities, but it was characterised by countless battles and loss of life (and much romanticising of the heroic generals and their armies). Crucially, the culture that was China was all but lost in this period.

Nick continued, 'Most organisations go through periods like China's Three Kingdoms where, for often quite good reasons, they split into "kingdoms" that become more important to the members of the kingdoms than the overall organisation. People build their departmental fortresses, lose sight of the bigger picture and even create a mythology around the heroes who do battle and win inside the organisation. The business loses its culture and fails to grow to its potential'.

---

**make the compelling business case for collaboration**

I've hardly ever come across an organisation that doesn't acknowledge the value it could get from better teamwork and collaboration across its 'kingdoms'.

But everyone is super busy, so you need to find a way to be heard above the noise of day-to-day work.

---

> The secret isn't in pitching the upsides of life beyond silo thinking. It's in creating a business case—a return on investment for solving real, tangible business-blocking problems that bother the leaders of the biggest internal divisions.
>
> Here are five common reasons why even the most cynical leaders will be strong advocates for a one-team approach:
>
> ▶ Cost and time overruns on important (and expensive) business improvement initiatives such as new information systems and sales channels restructures.
>
> ▶ Frustrated customers who are either leaving or complaining publicly.
>
> ▶ The duplication, reworking or repetition of mistakes.
>
> ▶ Delays in getting new products, services or policy initiatives into the market.
>
> ▶ Breakdowns or inefficiencies in supplier and distribution alliances.
>
> These are the pain points in an organisation that will get attention, and these are the ones that 'think one team' targets with well-planned and executed ninety-day initiatives sponsored by divisional leaders and driven by advocates. Where are the pain points in your business?

## fast forward

Nick would experience the realities of the O'Donnell's kingdoms a few days later at the quarterly budget review meeting. There would be fewer arguments outside an English football game: even with Nick as an obvious outside observer, a conversation between two staff members from Sales and Operations became so heated that an offer to sort it out in the car park was almost taken up.

Many a legendary story in O'Donnell's had its birth in these regular budget review meetings, which pit one department or function against another and became a battle for survival, and at times an opportunity to bludgeon an unsuspecting manager into giving up some of their budget.

A favourite story of many was when Ron Grisham found himself the target for blame over cost overruns on a project to install new enterprise software for the Sales team. Despite Ron's order to use an out-of-the-box solution, the IT solutions architect, for all the right reasons, engaged the Sales team to find out whether customisation would help to better meet their needs. This added an extra half a million dollars to the project (and probably saved twice that in rework), which Ron unpleasantly discovered during a review meeting. He later had strips torn off him by Charles, who immediately commissioned a review by his former consulting firm of the systems administration function.

Two consultants duly arrived the following Monday and spent two weeks on an audit. Not surprisingly, the solutions architect did everything possible to explain all the work processes while one of the consultants meticulously recorded and the other — who appeared to be a trainee of sorts — mostly just observed what was happening.

At the end of the two weeks, Ron was told to fire the solutions architect on the spot and replace him with the second consultant, who now had a perfectly documented manual for doing the job that he had been offered a fortnight earlier.

On inquiring by Charles whether the person had the skills, Charles smiled menacingly at Ron and replied, 'I wouldn't worry about that unless two guys start auditing your job'.

## hitting the spot

'The Three Kingdoms sounds like our manufacturing plant with the three jelly bean lines', commented Emma. She didn't intend to be malicious but it roused Judith, who observed dryly, 'and I think we have some bigger kingdoms when we look at Sales, Operations and Corporate'.

'Can't disagree with that', replied Ron to Judith's bemusement.

'Are there other kingdoms in O'Donnell's?' Jenny asked, hoping to flush out some hidden truths.

Donna Smart, a talented Team Leader in Information Technology, rattled off one area after another: 'Purchasing, Payroll, Customer Services, Production Planning, Marketing, Quality Systems, Accounts Receivable, New Products, IT, et cetera, et cetera'.

'And then cut it the other way', added Max, a Business Analyst. 'We've got the board, then the executive, then their direct reports—who are sort of a management group—then team leaders, operations staff and contractors. The boundaries are pretty thick between those levels'. Just about everyone nodded.

Nick continued. 'The Three Kingdoms is a useful metaphor because it helps us to see that organisations are almost genetically programmed to split into kingdoms or silos, and it stays that way until all the leaders—from CEO to Team Leader—deliberately think and act differently.'

He paused to make a crucial point.

'It's important to understand that there's nothing wrong with creating distinct business units or divisions. Business divisions and teams perform better and move faster when they have clear accountability, but when they do this in isolation from each other it creates a slow, inefficient business that can't respond quickly to change.

'When I advocate for a one-team approach it's absolutely not about forming one big department or doing some sort of silo demolition. That's a recipe for disaster. Instead it's about punching holes in the silos and doing exactly what's needed in a business environment of fast change and complex challenge.'

He paused again to make sure everyone was still following.

'And that's to create a culture of what we call "nimble, connected teams", where every team is accountable for being a high-performing team and for collaborating and co-creating with others.'

---

**nimble, connected teams**

The old truism, 'If in doubt, restructure' still dominates the conversations of so many management teams, who live in hope that adaptability and agility will come from tweaking the business structure. It keeps them busy but ignores the lost productivity every time they reassemble people into 'the perfect structure'.

I'm convinced that the organisation structure of the future will match what you see today in flexible, high-performing organisations in special military and emergency services.

This is a one-team model of 'nimble, connected teams'. These teams operate within the framework of shared tools and principles, which gives them enormous performance advantages in times of rapid and unpredictable change.

Look at your own organisation and ask, 'Is structure the key, or is it the capability to drive business performance and learning through nimble, connected teams?'

---

## and then along came joe

Thousands of kilometres away at London's Heathrow airport, Joe Narella, a second-generation Australian born of Italian immigrants, was waiting in the Qantas lounge to board his flight to Sydney where he was to commence his new role as Customer Services Executive for O'Donnell's Jelly Bean Company.

Headhunted by a prestigious executive recruitment firm, he'd been interviewed by Charles via videoconference and offered the job that would allow him to return to Sydney and to the young family that he'd seen all too infrequently since working internationally as an Export Manager.

It had been a whirlwind few days, but he was impressed at how quickly O'Donnell's had made its decision and he looked forward to meeting the rest of the team on his arrival.

They might have thought the same except that Charles had not involved HR in the recruitment process, so no-one apart from the headhunters and Charles's assistant Fran knew that he was on his way. Fran didn't get the nickname 'The Rottweiler' for nothing, so it was highly unlikely that she'd be giving up that little piece of information until it was in her best interests to do so.

Being blindsided about recruitment was something that Judith had become accustomed to, as few O'Donnell's managers bothered to involve HR in their hiring decisions, preferring instead to wait until the last minute and then demand that all the documentation be processed immediately. Ironically, even before meeting Nick Fox she had complained to Steve that managers ran their business units 'like their own little kingdoms'.

## it's not about teamwork

With the concept of nimble, connected teams understood, Nick turned to the compelling reason for O'Donnell's leaders to create a one-team culture.

Separating the group into three sub-teams, he gave each group fifteen minutes to create a list of the 'big questions' that needed to be answered to make O'Donnell's successful again.

Lists quickly formed:

- How do we get back the customers we've lost?
- How do we get new products to market faster?
- What's the best way to engage our people in the change that has to happen?
- How do we handle the day-to-day workload while transforming the business?
- How do we drive more costs out of the business?
- How do we better collaborate with our chain retail partners?

Each group had at least a dozen questions when Nick called a halt and it was clear that they could have kept going for a lot longer.

He flicked on a PowerPoint slide titled, 'Know Your Challenge', which was divided into two colour-shaded columns with the words, 'Technical challenge' and 'Adaptive challenge' sitting across the top of the yet-to-be-filled rows.

'How many of you drive a car?'

Every hand went up.

'Okay, let's assume that today when you go back to your car there's something seriously wrong with it.'

'Max has a Volvo so that's already happened', Jenny offered to laughter and applause.

'What would you do about the car?' asked Nick.

The same answer echoed from more than half of the group: 'Call a mechanic'.

Words rolled out under the heading 'Technical challenge' as Nick continued.

'So, would it be fair to say that the problem or challenge you've got with the car is technical or, in other words, there's a practical explanation and, even though fixing it could be expensive, you can find an expert who can handle it?'

Everyone agreed.

'Let's add a second dimension to this and assume that the mechanic asks who's been driving your car, and you explain that your partner has been using it for the past month.

'They tell you that it's been badly driven and that the problem will recur unless the driver learns a better way to drive.'

Nick flicked on the list of items under the heading 'Adaptive challenge' and added, 'I think you no longer have just a technical problem. This is a bit more complex'.

| Technical challenge | Adaptive challenge |
| --- | --- |
| Problem can be clearly defined | Problem is ambiguous and complex |
| Has a right answer | No right answer — lots of trade-offs |
| Can be resolved by an expert | Involves testing, exploring and learning |
| Can be solved step by step | Needs flexibility to adapt |
| Will enable normal habits to resume | Will involve shifts in long-term habits, beliefs and assumptions |
| Will result in less emotion and stress | Will cause ambiguity and 'squirming' |

'Whoa', exclaimed Jimmy, 'Houston, we have a problem!'

'What's different about the way you have to solve this problem?' asked Nick, amused at Jimmy's reaction.

'Well, you still need the technical expert', noted Steve, 'but there's no longer an easy solution, which means you're going to have to find a way to work through this with your partner'.

'How do you think they'll react if you suggest they need to learn how to drive your car differently?' asked Nick

'My wife would go nuclear', offered Max, before adding, 'You don't think it was my choice to buy a Volvo, do you?'

Everyone cracked up with laughter, which certainly hadn't happened in O'Donnell's for quite some time.

'Why would she go nuclear?' asked Nick as the room settled.

Max thought for a moment. 'Because she'd take it personally as criticism, and she'd resent someone telling her how to do something that she'd been doing perfectly well for almost twenty years.'

Nick saw his chance to ram home the point he wanted to make.

'How's that any different from telling your staff that what they've been doing isn't the best way to do it anymore?'

You could have heard a pin drop. No-one needed to state the obvious.

It was time for Nick's only lecture in the workshop.

'I believe the single most important management concept that has emerged in the past thirty years is this distinction between technical and adaptive challenges.'[1] His manner was now slow and deliberate. This was fundamental to everything they would do from now onwards.

'Let's look again at the list of questions you created to see if they're technical challenges.'

The members of the sub-teams didn't even have to look at their lists to realise that their big questions didn't have right

---

[1] R Heifetz & M Linsky, *Leadership on the Line: Staying Alive through the Dangers of Leading*, Harvard Business School Press, Boston 2002.

answers and couldn't be fixed in neat steps without emotional upheaval.

Nevertheless, Nick wanted to stress a point. 'How do you handle a technical challenge?'

'Find an expert', answered Emma, before adding, 'or solve it yourself step by step until it's fixed'.

'Exactly', replied Nick, 'so how do we solve all these adaptive challenges that don't fit into the usual way we work through problems?'

They discussed this for a few minutes and through open conversation three points emerged that would be fundamental to the way O'Donnell's transformed itself.

Nick wrote them on the whiteboard.

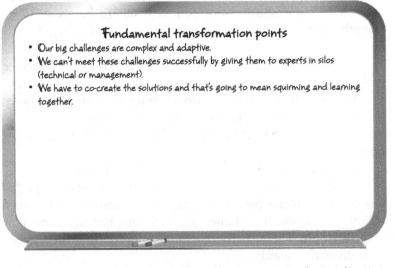

**Fundamental transformation points**
- Our big challenges are complex and adaptive.
- We can't meet these challenges successfully by giving them to experts in silos (technical or management).
- We have to co-create the solutions and that's going to mean squirming and learning together.

For Nick this was the breakthrough moment—the realisation that success or failure no longer rested within O'Donnell's technical and management silos. Instead it was about a culture where people and teams could co-create solutions to the many questions about customers, products, processes and people. That culture was all about 'one team'.

### learning together

Too many business leaders fall for the trap of treating their problems and challenges as technical. If you doubt this, just look at how management teams respond to the big, complex, ambiguous issues by restructuring, appointing teams of experts, or analysing and then analysing some more. They're looking for risk-free certainty and it's not going to happen in a fast-changing, disruptive business world.

Watch the nimble and effective leadership teams and you'll see that they align quickly (not perfectly), they collaborate (openly) and they learn (from successes and setbacks).

They move, they test, they co-create, they squirm and they learn while others are still planning.

Is there a lesson here for you?

# the five shares

After a short break, Nick scrawled the words, 'Five practices to defeat "Three Kingdoms" thinking' across the whiteboard and underneath wrote 'Think silos' and 'Think one team'.

| Five practices to defeat 'Three Kingdoms' thinking | |
|---|---|
| Think silos | Think one team |
| 1 | 1 |
| 2 | 2 |
| 3 | 3 |
| 4 | 4 |
| 5 | 5 |

'Is everyone familiar with O'Donnell's attempt to launch the green jelly bean last year?'

There were groans, nods and a few laughs all round.

Many years of consulting had taught Nick the art of quickly finding the best in-company examples of Three Kingdoms thinking and it didn't take too many chats with team leaders and operations staff around the canteen and car park to pinpoint 'Project Green Jelly Bean' as the perfect culprit.

Just about everything that could go wrong had gone belly-up with the attempt to launch a fourth jelly-bean colour the previous year. The green jelly bean was described in the national newspaper (with some accuracy) as 'tasting like cats' urine'; however, this gave Charles—who enjoyed any chance to strut his stuff in the media—the chance to deny the claims on the *Sunday* business program. Unfortunately, he met his match in a smart young journalist who enquired how he actually knew what cats' urine tasted like. Charles's answer still appears occasionally in television bloopers highlights (and was briefly trending as a top-five hit on YouTube), but the green jelly bean was gone before breakfast the next day and recriminations followed quickly afterwards.

Nick pointed to the whiteboard. 'There are five fundamental differences between "Three Kingdoms thinking" and "one-team thinking". Let's look at what these five differences mean in practice to see if they show why Project Green Bean may have hit the wall.'

## big picture or separate agendas?

Nick wrote on the flip chart that stood in the corner next to the whiteboard:

Pursue other agendas ├─────┤ Share the big picture

He explained, 'It's human nature that people are motivated and aligned to their most important agendas. In too many organisations there isn't an alignment to a compelling big picture that's more important than the individual agendas within the "kingdoms".

'You see this in places such as universities where every faculty thinks its program is the most important, or in the countless corporate head offices where arrogance is matched only by lack of awareness of what things are really like in the field. Think about the thousands of pointless bureaucratic rules coming out of head offices and the energy that goes into complying with them, or the wasted money on software that doesn't work because no-one asked the people who actually do the job!

'Think about the phone companies, power utilities and banks that you deal with. Do the people you contact in those businesses really know the big picture, or are they just one of the individual parts that don't know what the others are doing?

'We often hear the rhetoric about "whole of government" but rarely see two government agencies working together to solve a complex social issue. (Ironically, some do the opposite by competing for budgets for their own agendas.) It's crazy and very similar to the generals in ancient China who became heroes by destroying each other.

'When people genuinely "think one team" they all commit to something that they can't achieve individually but they can achieve collectively. That's a superordinate goal and it excites people and creates alignment.'

Nick handed out a sheet with examples of what he called 'above the line/below the line' behaviours and then sat at the table and quietly but firmly turned the spotlight on the group.

**above the line/below the line**

- We make decisions by thinking, 'What is the best-for-business decision?'
- We show commitment to the core values of the organisation.
- We show respect by considering the impact of our actions on colleagues in other teams.

**Share the big picture**

**Pursue other agendas**

- We make decisions by thinking, 'What is best for our department?'
- We don't really understand or care what impact our actions have on colleagues.
- We allow conflicting agendas to thrive between teams.

'Most of you were a part of Project Green Jelly Bean and if not, I suspect you've all had some similar experiences, so please read the handout and then take a pen, make your way over to the flip chart and mark the point between 'Pursue other agendas' and 'Share the big picture' that you believe characterises teamwork and collaboration between teams at O'Donnell's.'

They all sat down and looked at the flip chart. Everyone had drawn a mark as far away as possible from 'Share the big picture'!

## meanwhile …

Once a year Lollies on Parade!, one of Australia's largest confectionary retailers, decorates each of its twenty Sydney shops for its 'Into the Blue' promotion. Blue streamers and balloons, bright blue flags and even a blue carpet announce to the public that there are prizes to be won, including around-the-world travel, new cars (blue of course), hundreds of blue T-shirts and every imaginable type of blue lolly.

In the middle of every shop window a wheel designed to fit O'Donnell's sapphire-blue jelly beans in its numbered slots gives a stunning visual appearance as it spins and lands on a number that sends a lucky customer 'Into the Blue'. Tomorrow morning there would be queues stretching along shopping malls across Sydney. Into the Blue is one of the most popular and high-profile promotions in the harbour city.

Everything was ready for the launch except that over the past hour, while trucks were delivering O'Donnell's jelly beans to the twenty shops, the phone was ringing hot in the office of Tania O'Dea, Head of Marketing for Lollies on Parade! Angry franchisees demanded to know why they had received box upon box of bright red jelly beans to put in their Into the Blue window displays.

A livid Tania gave up trying to contact the O'Donnell's customer service people or the executives, who seemed to be in endless meetings. Being only a short drive away, Tania soon thundered through O'Donnell's reception, got directions from a still-smiling Susan, and headed straight into the training room, interrupting Nick's presentation and throwing everyone into confusion.

Four hours later, after turning the place upside down, the first run of sapphire-blue jelly beans made its way along the production line and into the waiting trucks.

'It's amazing what we can do when there's a crisis', commented Team Leader Sally as her blue team kept check on the line and corrected some minor temperature issues in the extruder. It was all hands on deck with even a few Research and

Development people helping on the line to fast cook the beans and check quality.

Mike drifted past in the background, wary of not getting caught in the crossfire between Purchasing and Operations. He could have stopped them from cancelling the order for blue colouring this week, which would have prevented the problems with Lollies on Parade! but usually customers put up with errors in orders and, in any case, his performance review was due next week and the savings would ensure that he hit his financial targets. And that, as Charles has said or implied many times, is more important than anything else. 'Maybe I'll even get a bonus out of this', Mike mused to himself as he sauntered off to the car park, leaving others to sort out the mess.

Jenny reluctantly postponed the afternoon staff meeting so that the Lollies on Parade! order could be filled.

---

### ask the 'one team' question

When was the last time you heard someone ask, 'What is best for the business?' during an important meeting?

Sadly, it's not par for the course in the corporate world or government for all sorts of reasons. For a start, there's competition for status and resources. In some organisations, if you give up something it can be seen as weak, so everyone holds onto information, money and other resources to make their 'kingdom' look best.

Irrespective of whether you're a team member, team leader, manager or senior executive, you have a responsibility to think about the big picture and not to push another agenda. The best way to begin doing that is to regularly ask the fundamental question, 'What is best for the business?'

At O'Donnell's, the way the senior managers deal with the consequences of Mike's inaction will also be an interesting insight into how serious they are about doing what's best for the business.

# back in the training room

With the blue production line spilling out sapphire jelly beans, Steve and Jimmy were able to convince a still-fuming Tania that she'd have blue jelly beans spinning in all twenty of her Lollies on Parade! window displays by morning.

When they reconvened in the training room, Nick enquired, 'How does what we've just seen over the past few hours and your experience with Project Green Bean relate to agendas and sharing the big picture?'

'They're both perfect examples', confirmed Jimmy. 'We have people who think they own the customers, so their agenda is to have control and to keep people out. In Project Green Bean they kept R&D away from the customers and even though the recipe matched all the specifications, people didn't want to buy green jelly beans because of both the taste and colour. We could have stopped the project and saved millions if only we'd known.'

Emma added, 'R&D has to share some of that responsibility because our agenda is to make the most technically perfect product. So I guess we're sometimes less interested in what the customer thinks than what science tells us'.

Ron mused to himself that none of the financial analysts really focused on Project Green Bean because their selective loyalties were to the red, blue and black production teams.

'That's an interesting insight', reflected Nick, 'and typical of the Three Kingdoms, where they created three governments—all with duplicated roles'.

'We do that', chipped in Rick, a Process Improvement Engineer. 'Each production line has its own accountant, chemist and marketing people, so it's not surprising that new ideas and best practices fall over because they can't bust through the silos.'

Judith added, 'Come to think of it, we actually recruit people to fit our kingdoms instead of the overall business'. It was a double 'aha' moment for the HR manager, who had also realised that they recruited for technical skills and gave little thought to whether people were open to ambiguity or the big adaptive challenges.

'So what should have been the big picture?' Nick asked.

'The same as we've just seen in the past two hours with the Lollies on Parade! crisis', replied Jimmy. 'Everyone aligned and working together to give our customers the O'Donnell's experience, which means great products and great service.'

Nick was delighted with the team's energy and insights but knew that he had to keep them firing right through all five practices, so he cut short the discussion, wrote the first practice on the whiteboard and moved on to the second practice.

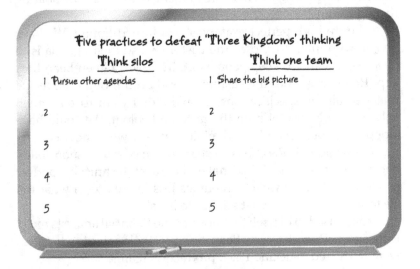

Five practices to defeat 'Three Kingdoms' thinking

| Think silos | Think one team |
|---|---|
| 1 Pursue other agendas | 1 Share the big picture |
| 2 | 2 |
| 3 | 3 |
| 4 | 4 |
| 5 | 5 |

## share reality or avoid and deny?

Next Nick showed the team a series of quotes from top performers in the fields of business, sport, emergency medicine and even an Everest expedition.

He paraphrased the common message: 'High-performing individuals, teams and organisations crave feedback'.

'Why?' he asked rhetorically before answering his own question. 'Because without it they can't learn and improve the capabilities to achieve their goals.'

He contrasted this with what happens when people think 'kingdoms' and compete against each other.

'You get low trust and it's much harder to get at the truth. You hear sugar-coated conversations in which people avoid the hard truths and put a spin on things. That means lots of blind spots, which put the business at risk.'

He referred them to the next section of the 'above the line/ below the line' handout and gave everyone a few moments to reflect on it.

**above the line/below the line**

- We put the difficult and controversial issues on the table and discuss them respectfully.
- We seek, give and welcome constructive feedback.
- We make the hard decisions and act on them quickly.

**Share the reality**

**Avoid and deny**

- The difficult issues are usually unspoken so they remain as the 'elephant in the room'.
- There is a lot of 'spin' on information.
- People avoid direct, honest feedback conversations.

Everyone marked their scores on the flip chart and again all marks were positioned well to the left.

## Avoid and deny |————| Share the reality

'Project Green Jelly Bean was a classic example of putting a positive spin on everything instead of calling it like it really was', ventured Max, the Business Analyst. 'Every department kept telling us how well its part of the project was progressing but no-one said what they really thought.'

'Which was …?' asked Nick.

'It was a great product that no-one wanted to manufacture, sell, buy or eat', replied Tracey, a Sales Team Leader, laughing at how ridiculous this sounded.

Nick knew the answer to his next question but wanted to see if someone was prepared to tell the truth.

'How did it get that far?'

Ron sighed and gave every indication that he was about to speak. Finally, he broke the silence. 'Because it was Charles's idea and no-one had the guts to tell him the truth.'

'Thanks, Ron', replied Nick. 'That's one of the most honest things I've heard anyone say for a long time.'

Ron flickered an embarrassed smile. He wasn't accustomed to being open in meetings or to having someone praise him in public. With a violently alcoholic father he'd learned at a very young age how to make himself invisible by concealing his emotions. It was a survival technique then and had been more than helpful in navigating the tantrums of the equally dangerous Charles.

Jenny was pleasantly surprised to see Ron's openness and wondered if perhaps he did have a future at O'Donnell's after all.

## more reality

In the pause that followed, Jimmy decided that the meeting could go no further without sharing the reality of his resignation speech to Charles and his discussion with Jenny.

'Is it a done deal?' asked Steve, breaking the uncomfortable silence that followed Jimmy's admission.

'Well, it was yesterday', replied Jimmy. 'But I'm disappointed with the way Jellicoe Candy Corp handled the whole recruitment process and, to be frank, the main reason I was leaving was because of Charles... and now he's gone.' He paused and looked at Ron, but decided against commenting on the difficulties that the Head of Corporate Services had created for him.

'Does that mean you'll reconsider?' asked Judith, pressing the point.

'Please give me until tomorrow. I'll have a final answer then', replied the rather ill-at-ease Head of Sales and Marketing, wanting to chat things over with his partner before making a final decision.

'Okay, let's meet after the staff meeting', suggested Jenny, expecting him to stay but still not totally confident that he would.

## cyb (cover your backside)

As the discussion resumed, Judith reminded everyone that each Friday an HR staffer emptied the quaint suggestion box that had sat for fifty years in the entrance area to the canteen. Over the past six months the two most popular suggestions were to fix the flood of internal emails and for Charles to do something that he would find physically impossible to do.

While the suggestions related to the latter were always discreetly shredded, Gary Fisher, the ever-suffering Network Systems Administrator (a great title for an awful job), had been working for some time on a strategy to stop the email war that was engulfing O'Donnell's.

Among the suggestions were to add another category to the emails after 'cc' and 'bcc', so that when people felt the need to copy others on an email they had to decide whether there was a good reason or whether it was just to cover their behinds. Judith's suggestion that 'cyb' be added to the system so people might show some courage by admitting their behind-covering behaviour brought a much-needed laugh to the group.

A few more minutes of sharp discussion and the group had grasped the idea that 'Share the reality' was not about blaming but about wanting and actively seeking feedback, being prepared to confront reality and knowing that a certain amount of conflict is healthy.

Nick kept things moving.

| Five practices to defeat 'Three Kingdoms' thinking | |
|---|---|
| **Think silos** | **Think one team** |
| 1 Pursue other agendas | 1 Share the big picture |
| 2 Avoid and deny | 2 Share the reality |
| 3 | 3 |
| 4 | 4 |
| 5 | 5 |

## share the air or stifle communication?

In a now-famous moment in the history of Project Green Jelly Bean, the former Head of Operations had managed to convene a sixty-minute meeting attended by fifteen people during which only three (including himself) spoke. Someone remarked later that there were more spectators at that meeting than at Saturday's national league football game.

Project Green Bean had all the hallmarks of silo mentality at its worst:

- The person with the loudest voice and the most power (or both) dominated meetings.

- There were few if any two-way conversations between the key players.

- Chronic hoarding of information was a feature at every stage.

- Plans were impervious to change, no matter how off-beam they were.

'We couldn't get a word in at project meetings and in the end there just wasn't any point in attending', commented an exasperated Emma.

'It was the same for us', revealed Donna from IT. 'Everything we suggested hit a brick wall of cynicism so there was no point. To be honest, we just put the project on the bottom of our priority list and nothing got done.'

Jenny was thinking about her own experience in a legal practice in which she had worked earlier in her career. The combination of a rigid hierarchy and personality clashes at most levels had stifled the creativity and energy of new graduates, who either learned to shut up and do what they were told or left to pursue their careers elsewhere.

She recalled that any views that even slightly challenged the status quo were discarded in a way that was probably more habit than intention. The most common phrase at meetings was, 'Yes, but...' and this deflated Jenny, who had been raised to share her viewpoint even if it was challenging to those in authority. She didn't stay long, but it was a good lesson in how not to run a business.

After a few minutes' discussion and reflection on the 'above the line/below the line' handout the group once again put their marks on the flip chart.

## Stifle communication ├──────┤ Share the air

The marks were again pushing hard to the left and everyone could see that O'Donnell's had lost the openness of communication and sharing of ideas that had characterised its earlier years.

**above the line/below the line**

- The lines of communication are open in all directions.
- We co-create by sharing thoughts and ideas about problems and opportunities.
- We genuinely seek and value diversity of views and approach.

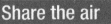

Share the air

Stifle communication

- Alternative views get dismissed or criticised.
- People or functions dominate the cross-business meetings.
- We are too guarded, which inhibits trust.

---

### buy spectators a parachute

'Stifle communication' has two sides to it.

The person who dominates the airwaves is probably the most obvious (and annoying) destroyer of both big and small teams. However, managers and specialists who quietly hoard information aren't far behind in the damage stakes because they take the oxygen out of the room.

The walls of corporate silos are thickened by managers and technical specialists who use knowledge for power or who simply won't speak up when it's needed. This happens inside businesses and also in so-called alliances.

When you see that behaviour, call it. These people are the airline passengers who see smoke coming out of the engine and say, 'Hey, it's not my responsibility'.

Buy these spectators a parachute and help them off the plane: they're a danger to everyone, including themselves. Don't put up with the 'oxygen thieves' either.

---

Nick suggested a short break before completing the final two practices.

| Five practices to defeat 'Three Kingdoms' thinking | |
|---|---|
| **Think silos** | **Think one team** |
| 1 Pursue other agendas | 1 Share the big picture |
| 2 Avoid and deny | 2 Share the reality |
| 3 Stifle communication | 3 Share the air |
| 4 | 4 |
| 5 | 5 |

# share the load or look after your own turf?

Most of the group used the break to visit the blue production team to see how things were progressing. While they were yet to discuss the fourth practice, 'Share the load', it confronted them immediately as they walked into the production area.

Research and Development staff were still there hours after their usual finishing time, people from Sales were helping to seal the special blue packages and maintenance staff from the black team were filling in for yet another person on a fake sickie. Two IT staff members were even arriving with pizzas to feed the troops.

'Is this how it normally works?' asked Nick, slightly tongue in cheek.

'Not likely', replied Jimmy. 'On a normal day it's nothing short of a union demarcation in this place. You get quite good teamwork inside the departments but no-one shares the load outside their areas. They don't think about it and they don't know what people do anyway.'

Nick recounted a recent experience with a large engineering firm where the partners and managers made an art form out of not sharing their load across or down through the firm.

They never planned or prioritised together, they made everything much more complicated than it needed to be and no-one ever thought to look left or right from their job to see what was happening along the line.

Clients wore the negative impact of the firm's silos and took out their frustration on the less senior staff doing the day-to-day work on-site. It wasn't until the top clients and then the most talented engineers headed for the door that the burning in the partners' pockets finally forced them to stop looking after their own turf and to share the load (and the big picture).

**feel the customer's pleasure and pain**

A sure sign of silo mentality is when people, particularly the end customer, are surprised or frustrated at their experience of trying to get things done. For many customers this means having to explain their story about the same issue over and over again to different people in the same business. Has it happened to you?

Contrast this with a one-team culture where there are few surprises because the lines of communication are open, people realise how their actions impact their colleagues and they act and speak as one voice to the customer.

The best way to encourage this behaviour is to focus on the customer and connect everyone to the reality of the customer's experience. To achieve this means bringing people together (face-to-face and through online collaboration spaces) to understand how customer expectations are being met, missed or exceeded. They learn about interdependencies between departments and issues can be addressed—provided that they're framed as learning, not blaming.

'Feel the customer's pleasure and pain' means recognising that everyone shares the same end customer and has an equally important role in the job of delighting that customer.

When everyone had returned to the meeting room, Nick asked them to read the next part of the handout.

**above the line/below the line**

- We treat colleagues from across the organisation as equal partners.
- We collaborate successfully on problems and opportunities.
- Our roles and expectations are clear and aligned with other teams.

**Share the load**

**Look after your own turf**

- Planning and prioritising mostly happens in silos.
- Inconsistent processes and practices reduce effectiveness.
- Tasks tend to be tackled by technical experts or management with little consultation.

After the team had reviewed the behaviours for 'sharing the load' they marked their scores on the flip chart.

Look after your own turf ├─────────┤ Share the load

The marks were again well to the left, but everyone agreed that 'Share the load' was much better inside the smaller work teams and departments than across O'Donnell's.

It was a fair point, and O'Donnell's was certainly not alone in that regard, but Sam and Eddie's surfing safari to Coogee Beach was not a good sign. In addition, everyone's pet hate, the almost compulsory late start to meetings while waiting for colleagues to amble in, was yet another indication that O'Donnell's had a long way to go to genuinely share the load.

| Five practices to defeat 'Three Kingdoms' thinking | |
|---|---|
| Think silos | Think one team |
| 1 Pursue other agendas | 1 Share the big picture |
| 2 Avoid and deny | 2 Share the reality |
| 3 Stifle communication | 3 Share the air |
| 4 Look after your own turf | 4 Share the load |
| 5 | 5 |

## share the wins and losses, or play 'I win, you lose'?

The final 'think one team' practice had been a feature of O'Donnell's culture since William and Walter shared a quiet drink with their employees every Friday evening to thank them for their efforts and to share the stories of the week.

In those days O'Donnell's really was one big team and everyone shared the wins and losses.

People still share stories, but more typical was last Friday's performance at one of the local bars by Jerry Porter, the Deputy Sales Manager known to all as 'Hippo' due to his thick skin, huge body and ability to drink more than most of the sales team combined.

As had become the habit on most Friday evenings, the people of O'Donnell's could be found drinking in their own department teams in any of the four bars within walking distance of the plant.

At the nearest of these drinking holes, Hippo was holding court with the sales team, while off in the far corner the finance team mostly sipped glasses of wine in contrast to Hippo's preferred strategy of one pint of beer in the hand and another waiting on the bar.

With a mouth full of beer nuts Hippo began his story in the loudest voice imaginable while the eight members of the sales team perched on their bar stools, eager to hear the latest gossip.

'You need to keep this quiet', he bellowed, completely unaware of anything or anyone around him. 'But our little Jimmy the Sprocket [Jimmy Goh, Sales and Marketing Manager, to others] is fishing for Grisho's head, and I reckon he might just have hooked up', he announced to more than a few blank looks.

Hippo sensed that more detail might be needed. 'Our illustrious Head of Corporate Services and his merry bunch of bean counters have a problem with the budget and they are going to get toasted at the next board meeting.'

He leaned in towards the circle of drinkers as if to share a secret, but without dropping the volume one decibel he announced, 'R&D are a hundred grand over budget already; we're two hundred over; and you can only guess what Operations are costing us with all their product screw-ups'. Hippo leaned back dangerously on his bar stool and laughed in a snorting fashion that flushed his already red face, still wind-burned from Wednesday's corporate golf day, to which he had scammed an invitation from a mate.

The wine glasses sat untouched as the finance team (and the rest of the bar) listened to Hippo's continuing exposé on the weaknesses, failure and likely demise of all of them. On his fourth pint in thirty minutes and with a fifth waiting on the bar, Hippo was warming to his task as the finance team filed out, leaving Hippo with the last words. 'Those grape juice drinkers will spread our conversation all over the plant by Monday. You can't trust 'em. They're the enemy, just remember that', he advised solemnly as he reached for beer number five.

'A gallon on Friday and you're set for the weekend', Hippo always advised his team. He was halfway to his target as the conversation switched to football and the all-important footy pool.

*  *  *

In the training room, Tracey from Sales marked the far left of the flip chart and wryly observed, 'It's like that golf saying, "every shot pleases someone". We've become a business in which people take pleasure in watching others fail. It's crazy'.

## Play 'I win, you lose' ├───────┤ Share the wins and losses

Jenny was pleased to hear that Tracey was much more engaged in the business than she seemed to be at the time of the airport lounge conversation she had overheard.

---

**above the line/below the line**

- We pay close attention to overall performance and results.
- We reinforce each other's strengths and contributions.
- We are quick to apply learnings and adapt to change.

> Share the wins and losses
>
> Play 'I win, you lose'

- We make process more important than overall outcomes.
- People look to blame when things go wrong.
- Disciplined and intensive debriefing rarely happens.

---

O'Donnell's had lost the ability to share the results of its collective efforts and instead had become a 'keep your head down' culture in which any mistakes had to be blamed on someone. 'I win, you lose' thinking was rife, particularly at across-the-business meetings such as the dreaded monthly Sales–Operations forum, where seeing someone else get nailed was actually a relief because it meant you were probably safe for another month.

---

**beyond the experts in silos**

Jim Collins in the business classic *Good to Great* used the metaphor of getting the right people on the bus and in the right seats to highlight just how vital it is to get the best people into an organisation and into the roles where they can play to their strengths.[1]

O'Donnell's largely has the right people (Hippo and Mike excluded for now!), but they're mostly experts in silos instead of people working for the whole organisation and its customers.

The cultural challenge is to connect the silos and help people to see and to value the non-technical skills such as teamwork, collaboration and co-creation. That will help to get people off their departmental buses and playing their part in the bigger picture.

---

Nick spoke as he added the final practice to the whiteboard.'When a silo mentality prevails, no-one shares the overall outcome. Instead of thinking about the business from end to end, people just look at their turf and breathe contentedly when they meet their own KPIs. They compete for resources and for attention and come to see things as win–lose. That absolutely kills the learning loop and puts the business at real risk.'

---

[1] J Collins, *Good to Great*, HarperCollins Publishers, New York, 2001.

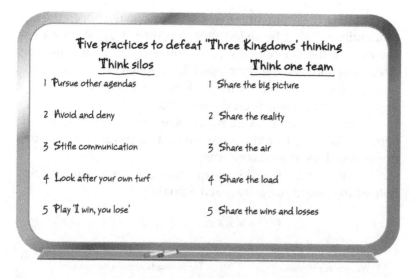

Everyone looked at the whiteboard. 'We call them the five shares', said Nick, 'and they're the essence of working as one team'.

## hopes and squirms

Jenny was thrilled about the rapport that Nick had built with the group and was eager to agree to the next steps, particularly anything that could be included in her presentation at tomorrow's staff meeting.

'How do you recommend we move forward, Nick?' she asked with unmistakable urgency.

Nick had reached this stage many times with teams and was always careful to make sure that the leadership team owned the plan, rather than handing it off to a consultant or transformation unit.

'A mentor of mine once said that the key to being an effective facilitator is to realise that the answer is in the room.' He smiled and paused for effect before reinforcing the point. 'The answer is in the room, and you are the leaders so let's find it.'

Splitting the group into four sub-teams he gave each the task of identifying what he called their 'top three biggest hopes and squirms' for the O'Donnell's transformation. After a few minutes discussing and creating their lists, Nick asked them to merge into two groups and to repeat the task before finally writing three hopes and three squirms on the whiteboard.

When both groups were ready, he invited Jenny to guide the conversation and to reduce the two lists into just three shared hopes and three shared concerns.

Jenny's natural style of questioning and summarising helped the group to easily reach a final list.

| Hopes | Squirms |
|---|---|
| We unite as one team. | The silo mentality is too ingrained to change. |
| We find breakthroughs that transform the business. | We don't have the capability to lead the change. |
| We future-proof O'Donnell's. | People will see this as just another change program |

Nick drew up a chair and spoke with genuine care and concern.

'These squirms are entirely to be expected and, of course, this is an adaptive challenge, not just a technical problem with a straightforward answer so we have to learn our way through this together.'

Nick recognised that the group wanted clear direction, but the inevitable rollercoaster of successes and setbacks that lay ahead also demanded the flexibility to learn and adapt. A traditional one-size-fits-all change management or leadership model just wasn't suited to this environment. A more adaptive approach and set of tools was needed and in Nick they had the perfect coach to bring that to them.

### where transformation begins

Initiating any type of organisation transformation is a complex adaptive challenge, so the big question is, 'Where to start?'

The answer is actually very simple because transformation is most likely to succeed when three conditions apply:

▶ First, the senior leaders are united around core values and the imperative for transformation.

▶ Second, there's a shared and effective method and toolkit for change leadership that's applied consistently across the various flagship change projects and initiatives.

▶ Third, there's urgency to move fast, learn fast and create real impact.

Put these three points together and you'll understand why the think one team method is implemented in three connected streams.

The first stream, United Leadership, builds the essential unity of direction, purpose and agreed behaviours among leadership teams.

The second stream, Cohesive Teams, ensures that teams are set up for success by instilling clarity of purpose, and an effective operating rhythm of alignment, collaboration and learning. This is an essential foundation because it provides understanding of the one team principles and tools, and there is little chance of teamwork between teams if there isn't strong teamwork within teams.

The third stream, One Team Culture, embeds a one team toolkit and approach into the business change initiatives and throughout the enterprise.

These streams are implemented in daily operations with ninety-day cycles to build capability and deliver business results at the same time. The ninety days creates focus, urgency and credibility in the business because people see direct results from applying one-team tools and practices.

Let's see how this plays out in O'Donnell's as they learn about the magic of the 'Align–Collaborate–Learn' loop and launch their transformation.

Nick was clear and confident in describing the way forward.

'From my experience there are three actions that will build the momentum and set us up for success.

'First is United Leadership, which starts by getting clear direction and strong collaboration among the Executive Team. We do that in a ninety-day program and then we can cascade the same approach into each divisional leadership team.

'Second is Cohesive Teamwork, which means getting a shared language and set of team tools and then embedding that approach across all the Divisional Leadership Teams and flagship change projects.

Third is about One Team Culture and that means engaging everyone in O'Donnell's to get on board with the transformation and the first flagship project. Let's call it "The Big Jelly Bean Team Project" and the ninety-day deliverable is a transformation plan that's been co-created with the whole workforce.'

Nick summarised the 'think one team' implementation plan on the whiteboard.

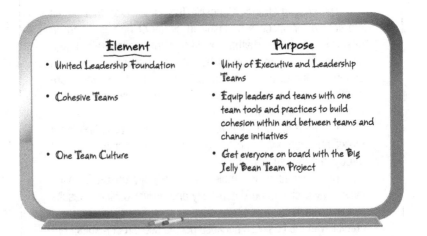

| Element | Purpose |
|---|---|
| • United Leadership Foundation | • Unity of Executive and Leadership Teams |
| • Cohesive Teams | • Equip leaders and teams with one team tools and practices to build cohesion within and between teams and change initiatives |
| • One Team Culture | • Get everyone on board with the Big Jelly Bean Team Project |

He concluded by handing over to Jenny and suggesting that she use the final half hour to confirm any actions leading up to or following the staff presentation.

He sat back and listened to a conversation sprinkled with the words of united leadership, collaboration, and learning and squirming together.

It was a good sign that O'Donnell's was again beginning to speak and act as one.

# engagement begins

It was 4 pm on Thursday and O'Donnell's staff had been arriving at the canteen for the past fifteen minutes.

Mingling in familiar groups and sharing bits of gossip, some staff were even taking a few bets about what Jenny O'Donnell would say. The smart money was on the double of Charles being sacked and some serious redundancy pain.

---

**engage early and often**

The best leaders of change all have one thing in common: they make a habit of engaging early and often with staff, colleagues and stakeholders.

Unfortunately, the former Chief Executive of O'Donnell's was too self-important to engage his staff early or often and the business was paying the price in low morale and productivity.

---

*(continued)*

---

**engage early and often** *(cont'd)*

That was about to change as Jenny set out to answer the three questions that most staff wanted answered:

► Where are we heading?

► Why is that the right direction for the company and for me?

► How can I play a meaningful part?

Reflect for a moment: are you and your team aligned about what is important, why it is important and what part each team member can play?

---

People squeezed into every spare space in the canteen as Jenny stood at a lectern and warmly welcomed them and thanked them for coming.

A single card rested on the lectern, written in Jenny's classical-style handwriting.

O'Donnell's Jelly Bean Company values:
• delighted customers
• a passionate team
• a respected business

William would be proud to know that Jenny was bringing O'Donnell's back to its roots.

For half an hour there was not a murmur as she painted the story of O'Donnell's from the earliest days in the kitchen in Birchmore Street to where it was today. More than one long-serving employee hid a tear as Jenny described what O'Donnell's meant to her father and uncle, and how William had brought her up to live by the principles that framed her speech today. It was a deeply personal presentation that connected with people.

'O'Donnell's is not the business it once was, and it is not the business we want it to be. The reality is that we have lost customers and profitability, but more importantly, we have lost our passion for the business and our resilience to face the challenges head on.'

She paused and looked out at the sea of receptive faces.

'We used to be a team. We worked together, we played together and we succeeded together.

'It is my intention, with your help, to lead O'Donnell's back to a position where we and our customers know that they are dealing with the best team in the business.'

Applause erupted across the canteen, and even Hippo was moved to clap and nod his approval.

'That started as of yesterday when the board asked for and received the resignation of the Chief Executive Officer.'

'Jackpot', exclaimed a loud voice from near the back, as cheering broke out across the canteen and the winners of the bets, including the owner of the voice, started plotting how to spend their spoils.

Jenny wished it hadn't come to this and remained impassive until the noise died away. She wondered what the response might be to her next statement.

'I am now Chief Executive and will remain so for as long as the board sees that I am the best person to lead this great company.'

More applause reassured her that at least for the time being, this was a move that would galvanise most of O'Donnell's workforce.

'I am not going to go into detail about why Charles was asked to resign because that is unnecessary. I will simply say that the business needs a different leadership style and therefore the decision has been made.'

Jenny dropped her voice slightly, 'There will be many changes and some pain because there are realities about this business that are not nice. Despite the short-term financial issues, I am convinced that this business has stalled because of our culture, not because of our products.

'There are people in this room who think the competition is inside the business and who are more interested in their own agendas than O'Donnell's. If that's you, then you have a short amount of time in which to change. If you don't change, there will be no place for you here.'

Her extended pause gave the line even greater effect. She meant it and no-one in the room doubted her determination to see it through.

'We can, and will, transform this company so that we again delight our customers and put fear into our competitors. To do that we must stop thinking and acting in department silos and start using our collective intelligence, skills and relationships to our advantage. Therefore, from tomorrow', she gestured in Nick's direction, 'with the help of Nick Fox and his team, we begin the transformation of O'Donnell's and the centrepiece of that will be to create a refreshed and reinvigorated culture in which everyone is committed to working as one'.

Jenny explained that the O'Donnell's executives would immediately commence a ninety-day initiative to sign off on a new business strategy and create the dynamics for a high-performing team.

Over the same period, a cross-functional group of team leaders would be trained by Nick Fox and his team as leaders and advocates of the think one team method. They would engage with staff to gather data and information that would help to develop the mindset and capabilities needed for the transformation of O'Donnell's, in which everyone would play a vital part.

Jenny took a handful of questions before again thanking everyone and closing the meeting.

---

**create your engagement platforms**

Bringing people together for face-to-face conversations with leaders and colleagues is a great way to generate real one-team momentum; however, most businesses are too busy, too big or too dispersed across locations to do this often, if at all.

That's why it's essential to create a variety of platforms on which to engage people within and between teams. These can include meetings, workshops and online collaboration and communication spaces and they are an excellent way to break down the barriers to communication in the corporate world.

One of the keys to being nimble and adaptive is to create and use these platforms to engage early and often with staff, colleagues and business partners. Have you got your platforms set up and working?

---

As people shuffled out of the canteen there was a new mood at O'Donnell's. Nick sensed it and so did Jimmy Goh—he was definitely staying in whatever role Jenny wanted him to play.

chapter 6

# united leadership

Jenny O'Donnell had been in business long enough to know that there was no magic wand for creating a high-performing and united Executive Team.

Even accounting for dismal leadership—like Charles had demonstrated—there are many reasons why leadership teams struggle to work cohesively and productively. Workload, conflicting priorities, unclear purpose and egos are just a few of the most common.

Nick sat opposite Jenny in the boardroom. Two hours lay ahead of them, during which they intended to leave no stone unturned to establish the foundation for a high-performing and collaborative leadership team.

## united leadership team foundation

From the scheduled kick-off next week, the Executive Team would be coached by Nick and his colleague, Jess McLeay, over a ninety-day period to establish the foundation of alignment, collaboration and shared learning that would be essential to leading the transformation.

Their activities would roll out over three stages:

1   A *warm-up* to assess team dynamics, and to ensure the readiness of participants and coaches.

2   An *induction workshop* to fully understand the think one team method, to strengthen relationships and to define direction and team operating rhythm.

3   A *workout* featuring deliberate practice to reinforce day-to-day leadership and team habits.

Jenny and Nick had important issues to address before the program began and first cab off the rank was the membership and structure of the team.

---

**make the tough call on team membership**

Arguably the single most common and damaging mistake made by new leaders is the selection or retention of the members of the leadership team. Too many resist making the tough call of moving people out of the team or bringing in others, and instead just allow the team to form based on the pre-existing organisational chart.

Jenny may already be set up to fail if she isn't willing to make the tough call about her team.

---

## the team: right purpose, right people?

Nick had no intention of commenting on the technical capabilities of individual executives but he would challenge Jenny in two specific areas.

He began with a suitably broad question: 'What is your view on the core purpose of the Executive Team?' he asked

She replied in an instant. 'The team must drive the transformation.'

Nick was relieved. The newly-appointed CEO got the reality that Executive Teams should only do what others can't. It was a nice change from the many CEOs who let their teams get bogged down with overloaded agendas, energy draining meetings and a sense of powerlessness to make real business-changing decisions.

Nick took aim with a blunt if not leading second question: 'Is this the team that can successfully land the transformation?'

Jenny shifted a little in her chair. This wasn't easy but she'd been thinking about it ever since the board offered her the job.

'No', was the definitive answer.

Nick waited for her to fill the silence.

'I'm mindful that we need to do a lot of work on the business strategy', she explained thoughtfully, 'but I see at least four weaknesses in the team and I intend to address them immediately'.

'Do you want to walk me through them?' asked Nick, assuming that Jenny would benefit from testing her thinking.

Over the next thirty minutes she laid out the planned changes to the Executive Team.

Jimmy would lose Marketing to focus totally on Sales. The reason was obvious: developing the sales channels was mission critical to success in the short and long term and needed full-time executive attention and accountability.

O'Donnell's was behind its competitors in Marketing and losing ground at pace; therefore, a new skillset was needed urgently. Jenny had already identified a top-flight Chief Marketing Officer (CMO) and an offer would be made shortly.

The second change was to move Research and Development into Marketing, which meant removing Emma from her Executive role. It was the right move to embed the customer experience into product development, and the new CMO, Andrea Matthews, would also be an ideal mentor for Emma's development.

Third was to create a Transformation Executive role, which Judith would move into, while an experienced operational HR person would fill her current role and report to Judith. For Jenny the transformation was a people and culture challenge, and while symbolic only, she would also drop the HR term and call the division 'Capability and Culture'.

Fourth was to narrow Ron Grisham's role to just Finance and Analytics. He would remain on the Executive Team subject to performance standards being met. Donna Smart from IT would join the team because of the role she could play as a champion of collaboration across the silos.

It would be a much stronger team, particularly as Joe Narella had also hit the ground running and was working brilliantly with both Steve and Jimmy to address some long-standing weaknesses in customer service and relationships.

With the team purpose and membership settled, Jenny and Nick used the remaining time to make sure they were aligned on key issues about the team dynamics and operating model to include in the United Leadership kick-off.

In ninety days they would look back on the conversation and realise that having the right people on the team and being deliberate about setting the foundation for Executive Team performance quickly pays dividends in every part of the business.

---

**warm-up—get people ready to learn**

Getting people ready to learn is half the battle, which is why I always advocate having a warm-up period in any one-team program.

Here are three things to do if you're planning to boost unity and performance in your leadership team:

▶ *First, build trust between the team members and the facilitator(s).* This is fundamental to creating an environment of openness and challenge.

▶ *Second, collect baseline data on team dynamics.* We use a United Leadership Team Survey to get feedback from a range of employees, and team style profiling tools such as the Team Management Profile (www.tmsoz.com).

---

> ▶ *Third, use an online space for pre-workshop briefings, collaborating on problems and opportunities, and doing quick debriefs.*
>
> The warm-up is vital because it sets up the expectations and ensures that people arrive at the next stage with the right attitude and understanding.

## the induction workshop

The Executive Team set aside two days off-site for the induction workshop, which Nick and Jess opened with a slide highlighting the five outcomes expected from the ninety days of activities.

90 days of activities — the five expected outcomes

1 stronger alignment on vision, purpose and priorities (Share the big picture)

2 greater openness and trust to have the robust conversations (Share the reality)

3 breakthrough ideas that transform the business (Share the air)

4 confidence in the team operating model (Share the load)

5 faster learning and ability to adapt (Share the wins and losses)

Early in the workshop the Team received the feedback from the United Leadership Team Survey.

'What does an Index of 40 mean?' asked Joe Narella, looking at the single score highlighted at the bottom of the twenty items that described team behaviours and practices.

'Put simply, it tells us the percentage of employees who believe that the Executive Team displays the united leadership behaviours and practices consistently.'

Joe nodded. He was accustomed to the concept of Net Promoter, which puts customer experience into a single number. He supported the idea of a similar index for leadership behaviours and could see the value and power of that single score to mobilising action and tracking progress.

## get the ACL and spin it at the right speed

Jess showed an alternative presentation of the Survey that immediately brought home the task that faced them over these two days and beyond.

| | | |
|---|---|---|
| align | share the big picture | Index 28 |
| collaborate | share the reality | Index 22 |
| | share the air | Index 52 |
| | share the load | Index 57 |
| learn | share the wins and losses | Index 39 |

The low scores on both share the big picture and share the reality highlighted where the initial work needed to be done. The display also included the words Align, Collaborate and Learn, which were to become the most important three words in bringing one team to life at O'Donnell's.

'You show me a high-performing team', said Jess, drawing on the whiteboard, 'and I'll show you this Align–Collaborate–Learn loop'.

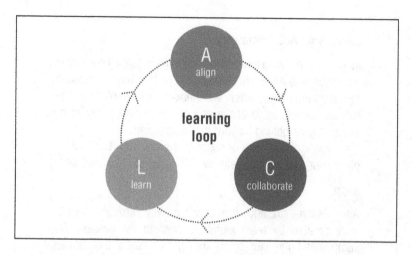

'As we move forward from here, you'll find that our whole focus will be on using one-team tools to get this ACL performance and learning loop happening within the team and to create the right tempo or rhythm for it.

'For example, we're going to use a Ninety-day Clipboard plan to get sharp alignment on priorities, a shared problem-solving tool to collaborate on the big issues, and a monthly action debriefing tool to help with learning and adaptation.'

Steve was familiar with the ACL concept and shared his experience with the team.

'We found that creating an operating rhythm of Align, Collaborate and Learn actions was one of the most powerful ways to embed the one team culture.'

'I guess we've been getting it wrong on both counts', remarked Judith, 'we haven't had the right alignment, collaboration and learning loop, and where it did exist it was too slow'.

It was time to roll up the sleeves and get into a stimulating and challenging series of activities that would establish the ACL framework for a high-performing Executive Team.

### create your ACL framework

In years past we would finish an offsite team development workshop with a leadership team and be thanked for facilitating the program. Now, after experiencing the think one team method, people leave at the end of the workshop saying how much they're looking forward to the program!

Here's a summary of some of the key activities that took place over the two days with the O'Donnell's Executive Team.

### align

An intense strategy workshop activity brought together work created by team members prior to the session. They summarised the key points into a tool called the 'Strategy Diamond'. This would be used to engage staff and show the connection between the big picture and their contribution. The simple visual would replace the overly detailed business plans that nobody ever read.

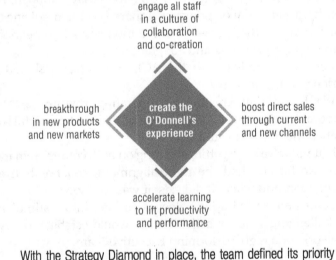

engage all staff
in a culture of
collaboration
and co-creation

breakthrough
in new products
and new markets

create the
O'Donnell's
experience

boost direct sales
through current
and new channels

accelerate learning
to lift productivity
and performance

With the Strategy Diamond in place, the team defined its priority actions using a Ninety-day Clipboard tool framed around four topics: Achievement – Development – Enjoyment – Partnering. These four core elements, abbreviated to ADEP, are essential for sustainable high performance. Vigorous discussion about the Achievement items helped to reduce these down to just five high-priority items that passed the test of 'Executives doing executive things'.

## collaborate

The Team Management Profile highlighted the team's overall style and potential strengths and derailers. This information would also be invaluable in choosing people for small, fast teams that would move quickly on key business issues. These are called FASTs—Fast Accountable Small Teams—and they are a brilliant way of connecting silos and empowering employees to break through the inertia of traditional hierarchies and business divisions.

A Feedback Circle exercise sensitively facilitated by Jess (with very clear ground rules) challenged each person to answer two questions:

▶ 'What would colleagues say is the single biggest strength you bring to this team?'

▶ 'What would colleagues say is the single most important thing for you to do differently to boost your contribution to the team?'

One by one the executives shared their insights and then squirmed a little as they heard what their colleagues really thought. This helped to boost openness and trust while also laying the foundation for the personal development priorities that each executive committed to work on with their coach.

## learn

The missing link for most teams (at any level of an organisation) is what we call 'closing the loop', which means regularly taking time to reflect, learn and adapt.

A key to closing the loop is defining a disciplined operating rhythm, which for the Executive Team included monthly team debriefs (using the Ninety-day Clipboard) and deployment of action debriefing tools into their business projects and activities.

By the end of two days, the relationships were stronger and alignment to the strategy and team plans was obvious.

Nick concluded with an observation from a colleague in the performance psychology field:

'People bring their best performance consistently in high pressure situations when they trust in themselves, trust in their colleagues and trust in the team operating model.'

The team still had much to do to get that trust while working under the dual pressure of 'business as usual' and the transformation, but they were definitely feeling more confident in themselves and their colleagues as they looked ahead to the workout phase of their United Leadership activities.

More on that later. It's time to see what a cross-functional team of leaders and advocates can do to set the foundation for a one-team approach to transformation projects.

# one team culture

The Lollies on Parade! crisis reminded O'Donnell's that the company could still move fast when the need arose, and Nick saw the same sense of urgency and teamwork in the cross-functional team that would launch The Big Jelly Bean Team Project.

The team comprised ten members who would play the role of leaders and advocates in a ninety-day initiative to engage people from across the business and define how best to embed one-team thinking and tools.

The One Team Culture approach would become the standard way that leadership and cross-functional teams tackled business-change projects.

## getting started

A feature of the One Team Culture approach is that, at the outset of the initiative, the sponsor and leaders define the scope of the initiative, the essential one team behaviours and practices and the desired return on investment. This information guides the implementation, including allocation of roles and choice of tools.

As Project Leader, Judith used the checklist of items provided by the facilitators to consult with each of the team members and with Jenny before settling on the top three items:

- a clear and achievable transformation plan
- enhanced staff engagement
- increased leadership capabilities.

She then uploaded these items into an online project tool which would provide a collaboration space.

## shared language and tools

In a two-day induction workshop the participants learned the language and collaborative practices that would play an important role in transforming O'Donnell's culture from poor-performing 'think silos' to the nimble 'think one team'.

They were constantly reminded that as leaders and advocates they must convey the spirit—not just the rhetoric or theory—of working as one team to engage and inspire people to cross the boundaries.

Around the room you could hear a new shared language emerging: 'share the big picture', 'adaptive change', 'align–collaborate–learn' and 'share the reality'.

Under the pressure of a challenging but fun business game, the participants surprisingly found themselves pursuing their own agendas, avoiding reality and taking a very narrow technical solution to what, on reflection, needed a more nimble 'learn and adapt' approach. Old habits die hard.

## sky to ground

Nick was confident that people recognised the basic concept of technical and adaptive challenges, but he needed them to understand what this meant to organisation culture and change.

On a flipchart, he drew a diagram that started with the familiar horizontal line from what he called 'linear technical' to 'complex adaptive'.

He then drew a vertical line to create four quadrants and wrote 'Sky' at the top and 'Ground' at the bottom. Filling in each box, he methodically explained the concept of 'sky to ground' and why it was one of the most important models for teams to grasp.

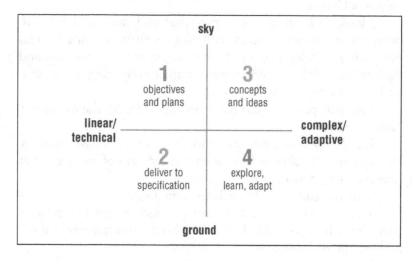

'The traditional way that we've introduced any change into an organisation is to start in Quadrant 1, and then move to Quadrant 2', he explained, pointing at the journey from top left to bottom left. 'In other words, we define a clear plan and then we implement it with minimal variation from that plan.'

'That's the standard industrial model', confirmed Donna, recognising this as the preferred approach of her team to everything.

Nick stepped back while Donna ran with it. 'I can see it already. The big challenges such as creating new products and lifting the customer experience aren't clear cut. They need loops of activity from concept to testing and back again. That's about moving backwards and forwards from Concepts in Q3 to Explore in Q4.'

'Shouldn't we be nimble enough to operate in all four quadrants?' asked Max, the Business Analyst.

'Absolutely!' exclaimed Jess. 'However, you will find that a lot of people want the certainty of Q1 to Q2, which you won't be able to give them when working through the ambiguous challenges.'

A lightbulb had just gone on for Judith.

'This model so easily sums up where O'Donnell's has got the culture all wrong.

'I look back on Executive meetings and can see that we've been tearing ourselves apart with half the team wanting to treat everything as being like a technical project with a clear plan and destination, while the others want to treat everything as adaptive and open for testing all the time.'

'Can you pinpoint the most telling effect on the business?' Nick enquired.

She slowly shook her head, not because the answer was no, but because she should have seen the reason before. 'We never take anything new from sky to ground.'

'Which means?' asked Nick encouragingly.

'The place is overloaded with partially completed projects that either haven't landed or are technical solutions that don't address the real problem.'

Everyone understood what Judith was saying and could have added their own horror story about how a mix of over-controlling experts in silos, poorly defined projects and lack of leadership had derailed the great company.

Nick had just one point he wanted to stress before moving on, but Donna jumped in and summarised better than he could ever have hoped to:

'We've got to stop criticising each other for what we do now. It doesn't matter whether we're working on new ideas or our established processes. They all can be improved.'

## four core capabilities

The remainder of the two intensive days were dominated by working on what Nick and Jess called the 'four core capabilities'.

Each capability played a vital role in engaging people and equipping them to align, collaborate and learn in times of uncertainty and ambiguity.

The first capability, Creating Shared Direction, used the ADEP model to set a ninety-day plan for each team. This model, shown in the diagram below, defines four essential elements for sustainable high performance: achievement, development, enjoyment and partnering.

Everyone was excited to create a business plan that didn't just focus on KPIs. In the coming weeks, they would learn how to use this model to improve their meetings, agree on development plans, and strengthen collaboration and partnering.

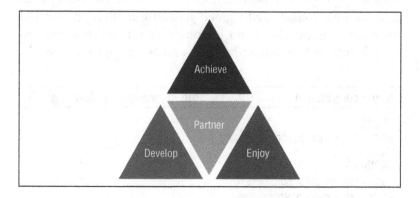

The second capability, 'Collaborative Problem Solving', brought small teams together using face-to-face and online problem-solving tools to tackle real business issues. It was their first taste of the power of cross-functional problem solving where people shared a common language and approach. The team easily identified numerous places (including in Sales and Operations meetings) where they could deploy the tool in the next ninety days.

The third capability, 'Team-to-Team Partnering', featured a challenging exercise to understand each other's hot buttons and closely define their expectations of each other when teams needed to work together. Jess and Nick interrupted occasionally to encourage people to bring a sharper reality and deeper listening to their conversations. They committed to using the colleague and team tools as part of their work in engaging people and testing the think one team method in the O'Donnell's environment.

The fourth capability, called 'Closing the Loop', introduced the concept of action debriefing and how to create a feedback culture. One of the tools, known as 'Mirrors', guided each person to assess their own contribution to the workshop and to draw feedback from colleagues. It created some squirm, but further reinforced that the ACL loop moved faster and better when people actively sought insights from others.

The 'Mirrors' tool is used in meetings and other forums to encourage people to reflect on their contribution. The rating scale features four colours, with green meaning a strength and red the complete opposite. Team members also invite colleagues to provide feedback on strengths and/or areas for improvement.

| forum contribution | red | orange | yellow | green |
|---|---|---|---|---|
| **engaged**<br>involved, contributed, not distracted | | | | |
| **supportive**<br>supported, encouraged others to contribute, explored others' views | | | | |
| **real**<br>open, honest, showed leadership, courageous when appropriate | | | | |
| **style**<br>style of communication and interaction suited the team's values and circumstances | | | | |
| **impact**<br>positive impact as would be judged by key stakeholders | | | | |

# ready for launch

An exhausted yet inspired group emerged from the induction workshop with a clear plan and commitment to make teamwork across boundaries the key to bringing O'Donnell's back to market leadership.

Of course, the induction workshop was the easy part. The hardest part would be to get people to break out of their 'experts in silos' mindset and share the reality of what O'Donnell's had become.

For the next two weeks the advocates prepared to engage staff, and they gathered the tools and resources they needed to measure and improve the current capabilities and practices at O'Donnell's.

---

**mental models are important**

The simple language and mental model of 'think one team' helps to shape behaviour, and to influence relationships and results.

Mike has already shown that mental models are important; however, when yours is to pursue your own agenda, then you act in your own best interests, which demolishes trust and collaboration, and you get disasters such as Lollies on Parade!

The five shares and ACL are proven methods, but they need a glue to hold them together. That glue is leadership and in O'Donnell's it will come from the unity of the Executive Team and passion of the leaders and advocates.

Without that glue the wheels will come unstuck under pressure.

---

# stop, start, continue

The advocates devoted one-third of their time for the next four weeks to The Big Jelly Bean Team Project.

Using online questionnaires and checklists, they launched a blitz of interviews, focus groups, 360-degree team and leader feedback surveys and the all-important chats in corridors to extract a total picture of what was really happening at O'Donnell's.

They operated in pairs and worked in their own area of the business half of the time and in a different area the other half. This ensured that employees dealt with someone they knew, but also that fresh eyes looked over each area.

Their brief was to create a current-state map of the business, based on the five shares and addressing three key questions:

- What must we stop doing?
- What must we start doing?
- What must we continue doing?

|  | stop | start | continue |
|---|---|---|---|
| share the big picture | | | |
| share the reality | | | |
| share the air | | | |
| share the load | | | |
| share the wins and losses | | | |

## share the reality

The advocates poured over information that was coming in from the questionnaires and conversations.

'Look at the Sales division ratings', remarked Donna Smart, pointing at a Team-to-Team Partnering Survey score of 15, which revealed a business unit that colleagues saw as having taken the 'experts in silos' model to the limit.

'It'll be interesting to correlate this with the Leadership Survey, commented Max, the Business Analyst, who was having a ball analysing the data. He posted a note to Judith, who was handling the confidential feedback information.

She later grimaced at Hippo's 360-degree feedback profile, which showed red-line performance in every key direction.

---

**I value your opinion ... but show me the data**

One of my colleagues saw the saying, 'I value your opinion ... but show me the data' on a wall in an international manufacturing business. It's a great way to remind everyone to go past anecdotes and opinions and instead get accurate information or feedback before turning the place upside down. This applies as much to a 'think one team' initiative as to any other business change.

Begin by measuring against the five shares in leadership teams and across the organisation so you know how and where agendas prevail and whether people are teaming effectively. Also consider using other validated diagnostics to assess progress.

Remember — I value your opinion on the collaboration and change in your business ... but show me the data.

---

The leaders and advocates developed a timetable for each manager and team to receive a detailed briefing on the feedback from the 360-degree survey and Team Partnering Survey.

For Mike, that feedback conversation would be one of his first share-the-reality experiences as one of O'Donnell's major destroyers of teamwork came face to face with the impact of his behaviour.

It would also be the first and badly needed dose of reality for some of O'Donnell's more siloed teams, who had hidden behind their own agendas for too long and used outdated KPIs to create the false impression that they were 'high performers'.

## simplicity wins

It's not a word that you'll find in the *Australian Oxford Dictionary*, but 'dumbplexity' seems to sum up how organisations have a habit of adding unnecessary and dumb complexity when what they really need is smart simplicity.

Rodney Williams from Research and Development and Andrew Ireland from Sales had applied the principle 'think end to end' to create a process map of how information from customers finds its way back through the business. They were now looking at how quickly and effectively complaints, ideas and compliments found their way through the business.

'Have you heard the story about the interviewer who asked the train-wreck question?' asked Rodney as he was collating information from a group meeting they had co-facilitated.

Andrew was absorbed in calculating average response times to customer complaints. 'No', he replied, 'what's that one?'

Rodney explained, 'There's this guy who works for the railways and he applies for a management job. At the interview he is given this scenario:

> You are staying with your family at a country hotel and decide to go for a walk along a high ridge from where you can see for kilometres in all directions. From there you see two passenger trains heading towards each other on the same line: neither can see the other. You're curious, so you look through your binoculars at the trains and then at the signal at the fork in the line. You realise from experience that the lines are not switched for the trains to bypass each other and therefore a crash will happen in about five minutes. You have a mobile phone, so what do you do?

Andrew had stopped checking the numbers and was waiting for Rodney to continue.

> The applicant just smiles confidently and says, 'I'd call the railway's emergency number and get put through to central traffic control and get them to electronically flip the switch'.
>
> 'Fine', says the interviewer, 'but the railway's phone system takes thirty seconds to run through the options like 'press one' to change your tickets and so on, and there isn't a number to prevent train wrecks so you're in a queue that could take up to ten minutes. Even if you then get through, the railways have

such a long line of command that it will take up to a day to get the okay to change the signal. By that time the trains will have crashed'.

'Okay', says the applicant, slightly shaken, 'then I'd run down the hill and manually change the signal myself because I know how the system works'.

'Sorry', replies the interviewer, 'but a new system has been installed by the railway's IT department and it doesn't have a manual override because it's guaranteed failsafe'.

'Alright', says the now-exasperated applicant, 'then I'd call Emergency Services and get them to contact the trains directly and also to send ambulances in case the trains do crash'.

'That would have worked', explains the interviewer, 'except that the Emergency Services communication centre is actually run by a telecommunications company that has outsourced its call centre to overseas. When you report that the trains are in Gladstone the courteous gentleman wastes valuable time before realising he has entered the wrong Gladstone into the computer. You, and more importantly the trains, are in a different state'.

'So, what do you do now?' the interviewer asks, confident that he'd completely thrown the bewildered applicant.

'I'd dash back to the hotel and get my son, Ben', replied the applicant.

'Does he know something about trains?' enquires the slightly confused interviewer.

'No', replied the applicant, 'but he's never seen a train crash!'

Andrew and Rodney laughed together.

'That's O'Donnell's customer service system isn't it?' said Rodney, banging the table to emphasise the point.

'Yeah. From what we've gathered, the IT guys have managed to create a system that's almost impregnable to customer complaints. We could be sugaring rat poison and even half a million people ringing to complain would be lucky to get past the phone queue to our two customer service people.'

'And if they did', added Andrew, 'their complaint would be painstakingly recorded on the complaints form, which is emailed automatically to the Customer Service Coordinator, who reviews it within a week and then raises it at the customer service meeting, which was last held four months ago'.

'And when a really pissed-off customer complains to the sales guys, we have to fill out the same form, which takes thirty minutes to complete and has to be keyed into the system because customer service won't deal with internal phone calls.'

Rodney and Andrew had uncovered just one of the many processes at O'Donnell's that had become so complex that it had lost the point of why it was created in the first place. Dumbplexity had to be thrown out or teamwork would be smothered by unnecessary rules and processes.

---

### common-sense simplicity

While Albert Einstein once said, 'Things should be made as simple as possible, but not any simpler', it seems that many businesses prefer the motto, 'Make everything as complex as possible, and not less so'.

Create a medium-sized organisation, get really busy and keep the people who are responsible for technology or processes as far away from the end user(s) as possible and you have the ideal conditions for this sort of dumbplexity to flourish.

The cure for dumbplexity is one team simplicity, and every business needs some 'simplicity evangelists' to seek and destroy processes that serve something other than their purpose.

Customers are the ideal simplicity evangelists because they're too often on the end of something that head office has created for 'administrative ease' or to save costs.

Vote with your feet when you experience dumbplexity as a customer, and ruthlessly drive it out when you find it in your business. Take Einstein's advice and make it as simple as possible, but no more so — because simplicity wins.

---

# who's the competition?

Silos don't just operate vertically, as Sarah Nuyen and Ed Gergiou discovered on hearing story after story of the way the senior managers in O'Donnell's keep secrets.

In the past year, three project teams had continued working on projects for up to two months after the Executive Team had canned the project. No-one thought to tell the people who were actually doing the work!

'How can that happen?' asked Sarah, a Finance Accountant (and one of the wine sippers), of two technologists from Research and Development.

'Simple', replied one of the chemists. 'Emma was on long service leave and when an executive is away no proxy is sent to their meetings. It was only when she came back and heard about the decision that we were pulled off the job. It's typical of the exec club.'

The reference to 'the exec club' made Sarah recall how Ron always came in from leave to attend the fortnightly executive meeting.

'I'd always thought it was Ron Grisham who kept everything secret about exec meetings', commented Sarah, 'but maybe there's more to it than that'.

Ed, the Quality Systems Manager, felt compelled to add his thoughts. 'I've only been here six months but since Steve Edwards arrived, he's always given us a briefing on anything from exec that's relevant to our operations.'

'Well, that's good for you', countered Klaus, the older of the two food technologists, 'but I think if you ask people right down the line you'll find that O'Donnell's is set up like a building with solid floors between levels and walls between departments. Steve might be the exception, but you'll find that there are massive blockages at team-leader level right across the business'.

Half an hour later, Klaus had recounted story after story of competition between team leaders. There was competition for resources, for attention, for promotion and for just being in control.

'How do you think Smithy was promoted from IT to Customer Service?' he asked.

Sarah shrugged.

'He was recommended by his boss because he was out of his depth which meant promoting him to another role and it was the only way to get him out of IT', replied Klaus with a smirk. 'There's at least half-a-dozen people in this company who just get shuffled from one place to another because no-one's honest enough to say they're not up to it. Team leaders just flick their problems to someone else.'

Sarah and Ed posted the conversation and reflections onto the team Idea Share. Many of the advocates added similar stories. The results of the questionnaires clearly pointed to the reality—that the silo mentality wasn't just between departments, but also between levels of the hierarchy.

'To be more nimble and responsive than other organisations', explained Nick to the advocates, 'we have to open up the lines of communication from Executives to Team Leaders to staff and back again. From what I can see, O'Donnell's has a culture in which people get their power and importance from holding onto information. That's a disaster because it sets up competition and slows everything down'.

Judith nodded. There's no doubt that one of Jenny's priorities was to close down the executive club and start trusting employees with the information they needed to make decisions. She wrote the word 'transparency' in her notebook.

The Big Jelly Bean Team Project was on track and Nick could already see the whole place was starting to think and act more like one team instead of competing against each other.

## executive team: doing the workout together

While the advocates worked on creating a clear map of the reality inside the business, members of the Executive Team continued to refine the actions that sat behind the Strategy Diamond.

Jenny wanted to be armed with this information to show the board, the executives and the whole organisation one big picture of the reality of O'Donnell's and its way forward. The time frame was tight, but the size of O'Donnell's and Jenny's and the advocates' commitment made it possible.

## *the workout*

For the Executive Team, the United Leadership activities were unlike any team development process they'd been involved in previously.

The constant aim was to improve the Align–Collaborate–Learn loop, which meant using the natural rhythm (and chaos) of the business environment to achieve outcomes, develop the team dynamics and operations, and relentlessly debrief, learn and adapt.

Nick and Jess worked closely with Jenny to coordinate the activities, which cleverly wove together field work, online collaboration and short intensive workshops and meetings.

Three items stood out for most of the team as being critical success factors.

### *simple models and shared tools*

Jimmy and Andrea, the new CMO, both had doubts at the outset about whether a simple one-team method and set of tools was substantial enough for a senior leadership team.

Concern soon gave way to delight at how effective the team could be by applying simple collaboration tools and using these in both face-to-face and online interactions.

'We've managed to move ahead on three big issues in the past fortnight that would have previously taken the loop of three executive meetings to discuss, refine and make a decision on', explained Jimmy.

### *using the ninety-day clipboard to drive the operating model*

Nick insisted from the outset that the team set its meeting agendas to only address issues that were defined as 'spotlights' on their

Ninety-day Clipboard. This sharpened the choice and definition of priorities and helped them go from jumbled information sharing to crisp and effective meetings. The first and most obvious example of fast and productive collaboration was the breakthrough in customer responsiveness from better cross-department links. The executives had done what executives should do and punched holes in silos that had remained impregnable for years.

### the new definition of accountability

Like too many leadership teams, the Executive Leadership Team had collectively been accountable for nothing. The real decisions had been made by the CEO (or occasionally by individual executives), so they decided to address the issue as a priority. Steve took the lead to curate the conversation, which targeted performance measures and accountability. Within a week they had changed the team's performance measures to focus on employee engagement and customer service where previously it had all been about only sales targets and financials.

The team members now act because they are accountable and not just spectators!

# what you accept you approve

One of the most important opportunities came in the form of the 360-degree feedback data on Mike, which quickly revealed the games he had been playing and the way that Charles and the previous head of Operations had allowed that to continue.

The extreme scores on the 360 ensured he was invited to meet with Judith and Jenny soon after the results were in. They were horrified when checking Mike's previous performance management reports to find that he had been rated by his manager as 'high' in almost every category.

O'Donnell's, like many organisations, avoided tackling poor performance, and the leaders failed to grasp the reality that whatever behaviours they accepted they, by definition, approved.

That all began to change today when Jenny explained to Mike in a very calm and assertive manner that he must radically improve all aspects of his contribution to teamwork or leave the business.

An angry Mike returned to his department and over the following hour confronted three of his colleagues about whether they had given him bad feedback in the questionnaires. Not surprisingly, he didn't tell them that he had tossed blame in their direction and he fully expected them to get the same carpeting as he did.

Mike was an expert at the blame game, but it's a game that's hard to play as the organisation opens the doors and windows of the silos and frees up communication. The team spoke with one of the advocates and they suggested a conversation with Jenny and a feedback tool aptly called 'REAL', which they used to prepare for a REAL conversation with Mike.

Just before 4 pm Mike, to his surprise, was invited to meet his three colleagues and Jenny for what descended into a bitter exchange as he dished out dirt and threats to all and sundry. His performance was way below the line of every one of O'Donnell's values.

Jenny knew all about workplace law and the risks of legal action; however, she was convinced that Mike had to go for the benefit of the whole team.

It was a 'best for the business' decision and he was gone within the hour, still blaming others and threatening legal action.

**you are the leader so make the call**

I read once that in any difficult situation the person who can best describe the truth without blame will emerge as the leader.

Teamwork across boundaries only flourishes when the appointed leaders seek out the truth and share it openly with people. This is 'share the reality'.

In Mike's case, the truth was that he didn't want to be part of a team and his behaviour reinforced the old way of doing business that Charles had epitomised.

In some situations you may have enough time and resources to try to bring Mike on board, but the future of O'Donnell's was at risk so the sooner Jenny confronted that truth and got Mike out, the better for everyone — perhaps even Mike in the longer term.

How leaders at all levels handle the Mikes of this world says a lot about their commitment to the big picture, to sharing the reality and to sharing the load. Jenny made that call because that's what leaders do.

Removing Mike had almost as big an impact on the morale of the workforce as Charles's demise because most people knew of his game-playing and saw Jenny's decision as a clear signal that this one-team stuff was here to stay. And most were delighted.

# chapter 8
# transformation — the new norm

After four weeks of intensive activity, the members of The Big Jelly Bean Team Project met with the Executives for a full day to share their findings and recommendations on how best to move forward.

To make sure that every attendee grasped the urgency of O'Donnell's situation, Jenny opened the day by sharing the realities that Steve had presented to an incensed Charles at what became his final Executive meeting.

---

### Current reality

1  Customers are buying other products instead of ours

2  We are unprofitable

3  Our divisions are underperforming silos that compete with each other

4  Employees are disengaged and leaving

5  Our business model is broken

---

She looked around the room at stern faces, all with their own thoughts—all with their own hopes and concerns.

'I know that most of you want more than just a job. You want a future. You want to be part of a winning team, not one that's scraping by on the strength of a fading brand name.

'Sure, we can cut costs and probably hold onto a patch of the market, but who wants to live their life just surviving?

'Fortunately, we have a second choice and it's not about being a victim of our circumstances.'

She flicked on the slide with the Strategy Diamond.

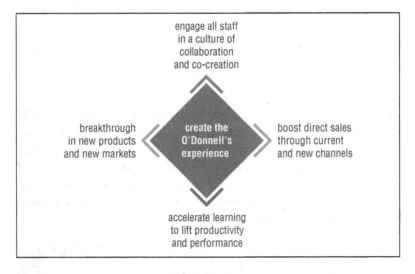

'Today I want everyone to recognise that this isn't simply a question of do you or don't you want to be part of the business or even part of the transformation. It's about asking, "Are we prepared to put this business and ourselves into constant transformation—to become so confident and so skilled at adapting that we don't wait for the market to disrupt us again, but rather that we do the disrupting?"'

No-one spoke as they all took in what that meant for them and the business.

---

**learn from the squirm**

Talking about disruption, transformation and unleashing the power of one team sounds engaging, but the reality is that it hits hard against the raft of protective and defensive behaviours that are natural human reactions to threat and loss.

Loss? There are countless books written about change resistance but they all boil down to one basic principle: people will protect themselves (even unknowingly) against change because they fear loss of identity, status, habit, control, recognition and admiration.

As O'Donnell's launches its transformation, it will be the power of simple tools and practices such as setting expectations in teams about partnering and enjoyment, working on shared problems, building rapport with partners in other teams and embedding learning loops and debriefing that will guide people through the continual change.

This isn't just about teamwork: it's about creating an environment in which people can learn their way together through uncertainty, ambiguity and disruption. All the while they will be challenging their beliefs and assumptions and feeling the squirm that comes with being in the learning zone.

---

# it's about attitude

Jenny asked the advocates to share the realities that they had discovered from their initial engagement with staff.

'We need to make some big changes', Tracey explained, 'but they don't have to be hugely complex or expensive because mostly they're about the attitudes and behaviour of all of us'.

'Simple and sustainable', thought Steve as Tracey continued.

She flicked on a slide and pointed to the list that appeared on the projection screen.

- share the big picture
- share the reality
- share the air
- share the load
- share the wins and losses

'It's about doing these five things brilliantly within and between teams, and we're well underway because these past four weeks have already shown how much we can achieve when we share the reality and share the air.'

Each advocate shared the mix of stories and data that they had collected over the four weeks. There were many examples of agendas, blame, stifled communication and turf fights that inevitably ended poorly for O'Donnell's and its customers. Time and again, however, they shared stories of successful projects and performance that revealed what happened when people worked across the boundaries, shared a common big picture and brought the five shares to life.

'Excellent', exclaimed Nick, eager not to lose the positive momentum that was building.

'We have two things to do: first is to engage every O'Donnell's employee in the one-team message and rollout, and second is to confirm the scheduling of the transformation projects.'

With so many bright and motivated people in the room, it didn't take long for them to create a schedule of engagement workshops timed so that O'Donnell's staff could attend without major interruption to service or production.

The workshops would be large group activities designed and co-facilitated by the advocates and Nick and Jess.

Involving the advocates as facilitators in the workshops meant this wasn't just another training course and it also reinforced their position as leaders of the one team initiatives.

The main ground rule for co-facilitators was that when negative things about O'Donnell's and its people were raised, the process had to be facilitated in a constructive way that finished by looking forward. It was a tactic learned from a sport psychologist who observed that the best coaches have really tough conversations, but they leave their athletes looking forward (instead of looking to blame or rationalise).

'We have many harsh realities to share in the coming months', Nick stressed, 'but that won't improve the business unless people see the leaders focusing on solutions instead of blame'.

## the first 'think one team' workshop

The first of the large-group workshops was held at a nearby conference centre and began with a team game designed to challenge people to work in small teams while striving towards an overall big picture. The game was like a combination of three-dimensional jigsaw puzzles and pass-the-parcel and, among mayhem and laughter, showed everyone what happens when people think silos instead of 'one team'.

After debriefing the game and linking it to the five shares the attendees were prepared for the main activity of the day.

Workstations had been set up around the room and labelled according to the five shares, starting from the left with 'Share the big picture' and moving around to 'Share the wins and losses'. At each station, data and information collected by the coaches was displayed in easy-to-understand formats on posters, and large sheets of flip chart were ready and waiting.

For the next two hours, small groups shuffled around under the guidance of the facilitators until flip-chart paper covered the walls. Items were recorded in coloured pen under the headings 'Stop', 'Start' and 'Continue'. Stars next to some items identified them as the 'spotlight' items to be given attention.

Two members of the project team—Donna and Max—stood back with Jenny and watched as staff milled around the 'Share the big picture' workstation debating issues, jotting ideas on flip charts and moving on as they were ready to engage with another group.

'Are we getting the issues out in the open?' asked Jenny of her bright and enthusiastic colleagues.

In the 'Stop' column three items had stars next to them.

**stop**

| | |
|---|---|
| ☆ | setting department goals and measures that set up internal competition |
| ☆ | making decisions without consulting the people who are affected |
| ☆ | management clubs (executives and team leaders) |

'They're being really open', said Max, looking further down the column at some of the other 'stops'.

**stop**

| | |
|---|---|
| ☆ | the 'cyb' emails |
| ☆ | the personality feuds between Sales and Finance |
| ☆ | blindsiding people in public forums |
| ☆ | playing solo when we need the whole orchestra |
| ☆ | trying to over-achieve and not finishing anything properly |
| ☆ | blaming whenever something looks like it will go wrong |

Jess and Nick conferred as people mixed, chatted, challenged, laughed, debated and did everything that you would expect of colleagues who were on the same team.

'It's building a head of steam', Jess observed as a burst of applause rose from a group near the 'Share the load' wall.

'What's that one all about?' asked Nick, his view of the poster obscured by Nathan Smith, the 195-centimetre tall former football star who worked in Operations.

Jess laughed. 'It says, 'Scrap the SLAs'.

SLA was code for Service Level Agreements, the dreaded contracts between departments that were brought in to improve the in-company customer service, but did nothing more than create demarcation and a weapon for one part of the company to use against the other. IT and Finance copped the worst of it as Sales and Operations demanded that their priorities be met, although more than once the positions were reversed as they were told to wait their turn because 'it isn't in the SLA'!

More cheering arose from the direction of 'Share the wins and losses'.

'STOP GOING TO SEPARATE BARS ON FRIDAYS!!!' was scrawled in capital letters across the poster, and a beaming Hippo burst from the group dancing with an equally animated Sarah, the wine drinker from Finance.

'Yes, yes, yes', chanted three members of the Sales team as 'Start getting Finance to work with Sales to monitor the budgets' was logged as an action in 'Share the wins and losses'.

---

### scrap the SLAs

SLAs are outdated technical solutions that reinforce power struggles inside a business and make collaboration and trust harder to establish.

If you use a formal service-level contract to manage interaction between two or more departments or functions, I'd respectfully suggest that you challenge the managers of those areas because it is they who are accountable for aligning expectations, delivering on commitments and keeping the lines of communication open.

Scrap the SLAs and replace them with genuine one-team Partnering Agreements that include expectations and the all-important Align – Collaborate – Learn loop.

---

The energy built as the facilitators skilfully shifted the attention of the whole group backwards and forwards from the big picture of the Strategy Diamond to the posters and flip chart in front of them. By late afternoon action lists were refined, priorities agreed upon and development tasks (with deadlines) allocated to cross-functional teams.

The next day an almost identical workshop with another group of leaders and staff showed everyone that O'Donnell's was ready to transform its business by dumping silo thinking and replacing it with the simple mantra, 'think one team'.

# chapter 9
# acceleration

## three months later

Every month Jenny O'Donnell assembled the leaders of O'Donnell's Jelly Bean Company to review progress and set the next month's priorities for transformation. It was a part of the operating rhythm and a great example of working as partners without the status barriers that had previously stifled communication and decision making.

Quick wins built the momentum and confidence for change as staff saw that O'Donnell's really could be reinvented without losing the parts of the culture that they all loved. There were still plenty of entrenched practices and heavy baggage to challenge, but as Steve noted, 'The drumbeat is getting faster'.

Transformation initiatives had been launched using ninety-day One Team Culture activities to create urgency and a one-team approach. As a consequence, staff felt genuinely engaged in co-creating solutions to these big challenges and problems. Engagement was measured fortnightly as part of 'closing the loop' and the score had climbed steadily across the three months.

Everyone loved the simplicity of the 'think one team' tools and had their own favourites.

Joe Narella was a breath of fresh air in Customer Service despite the complete disbelief from Judith that Charles had recruited a person sight unseen from the other side of the world. He was a total advocate for co-creation and took no time to work with Andrea to pilot a collaboration jam with customers that triggered a fast-growing online community of valuable advocates and evangelists for the products.

A reinvigorated and focused Jimmy Goh had an expanded Sales team firing on all cylinders, and for the first time O'Donnell's jelly beans were mixed together in cellophane bags. Innovative new colours and flavours, product shapes and some stunning promotional ideas showed what happened when Research and Development, and Marketing started thinking and acting as one team.

Steve led the disbandment of the production 'kingdoms' in favour of a more flexible arrangement where people were encouraged and rewarded for moving across different parts of the business. Almost miraculously, the underutilised improvement teams and project-management tools started to fulfil their promise, instead of being just one more O'Donnell's fad that didn't work.

'Think One Team' had become a new catch cry, replacing the ways of working that had frustrated staff, added to costs and slowed O'Donnell's to a crawl. Accountability for decisions was pushed as far into the business as possible and people became accustomed to being challenged about the performance in their own function *and* for connecting the silos.

Finance treated leaders as important partners and even created innovative reports that were helping to drive efficiencies and quick decisions, and under Jenny's leadership the executives opened the lines of communication and started acting like high-performance leaders instead of mediocre managers.

Importantly, O'Donnell's didn't fall into the trap of thinking that 'one team' meant making everyone dependent on everyone else. Quite the opposite. Where interdependency added value they made it work, but where it slowed decision making and negatively affected customer service it was avoided. It really was 'silos with holes in them', as Jimmy noted.

Each of the divisional leadership teams was well underway building cohesion and developing skills to coach the one team culture, which was not only giving them a framework for working together, but made team-to-team partnering so much easier now that everyone used the same language and tools. There had been initial reluctance from a few managers to using Ninety-day Clipboards; however, even Brad Drewett acknowledged their value, which was quite something for a man who was once described in a Sales and Operations meeting as 'never meeting a plan that he liked'.

Collegiate meetings with tight agendas and a focus on collaboration replaced the high-spin, high-blame, cross-functional meetings. A new language was emerging as people were heard asking one-team questions such as, 'Who do we need to engage?' and 'How do we build better relationships?'

Meeting rooms were stocked with posters and toolkits that reinforced the values and the 'think one team' messages of the five shares and Align – Collaborate – Learn.

Among all the changes, arguably the most obvious was the reception area. Susan still smiled, but the Rottweiler had chosen guard duty at another company and those stunning glass cylinders no longer stood as the perfect symbol of the silos in O'Donnell's.

The cylinders themselves remained, but now they were randomly filled with different-coloured beans, which reminded everyone to 'think one team'.

## chapter 10

# inspiration

## six months later, kowloon, hong kong

A Chinese junk bobbed in the wake of a sleek white ferry, the captains briefly exchanging glances as they plied their trade in the auditorium that is Hong Kong harbour. A fluffy white cloud hung over Victoria Peak as if joining Nick Fox in savouring one of the great city views of the world.

As far as views from hotel rooms go, Nick rated the one from the Royal Pacific Hotel in Kowloon one of the best he had seen, but most of the forty-plus Chief Executives in the room were more curious about the secretive invitation from the Asia–Pacific leaders forum, of which they were members, to spend three days together in Hong Kong.

Arriving to find a wide, open room, they milled uncomfortably around the perimeter, which featured multiple large plasma screens and white panels designed for writing on.

A table stood in the middle of the room with three glass cylinders full of large blue, red and black jelly beans, respectively.

From banks, governments, universities, mining, fast-moving consumer goods, telecommunications and hospitality businesses they had come on the promise of learning about, and experiencing, something of immense value to their businesses.

Hong Kong is proof that businesses no longer make money just from assets, and the mix of the attendees made it quite clear that the old boundaries of country, industry, age and gender were no more. With money flowing at the speed of light and ideas a dime a dozen, the banker from Shanghai, the mining executive from Santiago and the twenty-something hi-tech CEO from Silicon Valley were always looking for the breakthrough that could disrupt their industry—or someone else's.

It was now nine months since Nick Fox had landed in Australia with a plan to write a book and seek the inspiration to disrupt his own business. That had happened, but as is so often the case, it was something totally out of left field that delivered more than he could ever have dreamed possible.

He dismissed the nervous anticipation rising in his stomach and flicked the switch that brought his lapel microphone and the plasma screens to life.

'Welcome to "think one team"', he announced to the still-standing executives.

On cue, waiters dressed in crisp white jackets appeared from every entrance of the round conference room carrying silver trays full of brightly coloured jelly beans. Each tray contained just one colour: red, blue, black or green. Each jelly bean was the size of a bird's egg.

'Please sample one of each colour', Nick said, smiling, 'but leave the green to last'. He motioned the four waiters with trays of green jelly beans to the rear of the room, leaving the others in what quickly became a polite, yet eager, feeding frenzy.

Nods of approval. Groans of delight. Savouring of the taste explosion that is the O'Donnell's black jelly bean. No sweet anywhere in the world quite matched the O'Donnell's jelly bean at its best.

'Has anyone not yet tasted the blue, red and black jelly beans?' enquired a female voice from the rear of the room. The audience turned towards the sound.

A petite woman in her mid forties stood flanked by four waiters, each with a tray of green jelly beans. Mai Lee, born in Hong Kong and educated in London, was one of Nick's best facilitators, with a host of clients across Asia and the Middle East.

'Please take one green jelly bean and a tissue', she instructed politely.

The waiters pressed forward among the audience, followed soon after by howls of disapproval and muffled spitting into the tissues. Cultural differences defined the extent of the reactions.

'Ladies and gentlemen', Nick paused as they shifted their attention towards him. 'Today you will hear the story of the company that made those magnificent blue, red and black jelly beans.'

Waiters again moved through the crowd, collecting the green-stained tissues and handing out blue jelly beans to replace the taste of cat urine being experienced by the audience.

Nick continued. 'It's difficult to believe, but those disgusting green jelly beans were made by the very same company that made the other jelly beans, with the same people and the same production process.'

'Of course, your enterprises do not make jelly beans, but you do each face the same challenge. That challenge is to create a culture inside your business that makes success inevitable.'

Nick paused while the plasma screens each showed that phrase as a question in capital letters:

*HOW DO WE CREATE THE CULTURE IN*
*WHICH SUCCESS IS INEVITABLE?*

'Ladies and gentlemen, on the tables around the perimeter you will see that the waiters have placed name cards next to tablets. Please find your name card and tablet.

'Start the tablet and you will see a link to Think One Team. Please log in by choosing a suitable password and then watch the brief video, which will explain exactly why you are here.'

There was a polite scramble to get the tablets and then silence while people logged in and watched the video with headphones on. The video promised two things:

- First, that they would learn a revolutionary method for engaging employees, connecting silos and transforming organisations.

- Second, that in these three days they would be applying that method in a team with four other CEOs and their task would be to create a business venture that leveraged the resources, capabilities and networks of their collective organisations. Their company boards had given approval for this venture and expected them to report on the value created after ninety days.

The Chief Executives looked at Nick with a mix of apprehension and indignation. They were used to being in control and certainly didn't take kindly to being publicly blindsided by their boards.

'Yes', Nick announced, 'You are here to create something of value, something that your individual enterprises cannot create by themselves but can create by working together as one team.

'From that experience you will bring to your enterprises a way to create a culture that makes success almost inevitable.

'Shall we begin?'

## the 'think one team' experience

For three days the Chief Executives worked together to learn and apply the simple, practical think one team tools to a real business challenge.

On the first day, a presentation brought O'Donnell's, the jelly bean company from Sydney, to life in the conference room overlooking Hong Kong harbour.

Facilitated by Nick and Mai Lee, each team learned about the five shares and the power of creating Align–Collaborate–Learn loops.

At first they were noticeably reluctant to go outside the status quo and their own boundaries, even rejecting suggestions to engage people from their own organisations in the challenge.

Nick guided them through an activity that helped each individual to recognise the way they protected themselves from the risks and losses of adaptive change. It helped to open them to learning more quickly by showing vulnerability.

By the end of the first day each team of five CEOs had found a superordinate goal that met the three tests that their boards required. The requirements were that the goal:

- could only be achieved by working together as one team
- would create extraordinary value
- could be achieved in full or to a significant milestone within ninety days.

During day two they learned and applied the four capabilities of 'think one team' to move their initiative forward.

Using an online collaboration platform, they formed cross-functional teams from across their various organisations and coached them to align goals and performance measures using the ADEP model. It was an activity that caused most of them to reflect on the narrow KPI-driven model that dominated their enterprises.

The leaders practised the skills of curating cross-functional, multinational, intercompany conversations and surprised themselves with the power of shared language and simple one team tools.

Nick was enormously excited at some of the goals that the teams had set for themselves. Interestingly, most had extended the definition of 'value' to well beyond profitability and into community and nation building. For example, one team comprising a mix of banking, technology, healthcare and infrastructure enterprises had set a goal to transform the quality and access to healthcare in a selected region of South-East Asia by completely changing the usual channels through which doctors deliver services. It was disruption on a mega scale.

The debriefing at the end of day two revealed ground-breaking insights for the majority of attendees. While some initially struggled with the notion of small, fast teams, they now reflected on how their teams spread across the world were applying 'think one team' tools to perform and learn faster than these CEOs could ever imagine.

At the start of the final day a presentation on the O'Donnell's debacles revealed how teamwork across boundaries doesn't flourish until you create genuine partnering relationships with empathy, shared goals and aligned expectations.

Towards the end of day three, in the final interactive session, there was great cheering as each team lifted the caps from the tops of the cylinders of jelly beans, tipped the contents into bowls, mixed them together and then refilled the cylinders.

Like the entrance to O'Donnell's, the cylinders had been the ultimate symbol of silo thinking and poor teamwork. As the executives headed towards the airport, they were excited about their project, but more importantly they already saw how to unlock the potential in themselves and their organisations, which had been shackled by silo thinking.

Foremost in their minds was the realisation that from the tables in Hong Kong and the entrance to O'Donnell's offices in Sydney, the multi-coloured cylinders revealed that it isn't about big jelly beans, but rather about how to connect the silos to become a Big Jelly Bean Team.

## fifteen months later

It was two years ago to the day that Jenny O'Donnell, with a resolve to save her father's legacy, took over the reins of O'Donnell's Jelly Bean Company. Tonight she sat alone. Her choice of restaurant was more for nostalgia than the cuisine, although Doyles, the famous seafood restaurant at Watsons Bay with the stunning view along Sydney Harbour towards the bridge, could rate with the best. She was deep in thought as a huge white cruise ship slipped silently past, its wake slapping against the shore.

Lights twinkled along the harbour as they had done years before when Jenny shared her last meal with her father. It had been two days before her thirtieth birthday.

'Jenny', he had said in the rasping voice of a man with too few breaths left to live, 'as you know there has always been a plaque on the wall in my office with the three principles that I have lived by in my business life for forty years'. He paused to draw breath while tears welled in her eyes. 'I know that these principles are also important to you; however, there is one missing and I only realised it in the past few years, perhaps because I took it for granted.'

Jenny waited as her father coughed a hard, painful cough that would claim his life just five days later. 'When times are tough you need more than intention, courage and respect; you need people to share the highs and lows — to see a bigger picture than you can find by yourself. You need to talk and listen, to be honest with each other and to share the load. Sometimes you find those people in your family or your community, or in your business. I'm lucky that I had a great partner in marriage, another in my business and then a team of partners at O'Donnell's. I like to think of all these people as being just a part of one big team.

'For too long I took those partners for granted and in you I see some of the stubbornness and independence that I came to see in myself. The three principles are wonderful and I hope that you continue to keep them in mind.'

He handed Jenny the plaque with the three principles and she looked at them, knowing how much they meant to a dying man.

*Be clear about your intentions*
*Act decisively with courage*
*Give and earn respect*

'There was no space on the front for a fourth principle, so I pencilled it on the back as a reminder.'

Jenny turned over the plaque and written in William's impeccably neat handwriting was the phrase:

**think one team**

# part II

# the think one team method

It is both natural and desirable for organisations to separate into smaller units such as divisions, departments and teams. This separation gives focus, specialisation and ownership, which offers the promise of greater efficiency and effectiveness, faster decision making and increased engagement for the people involved.

Unfortunately, this separation into units often comes at an unacceptable cost.

Instead of performance and growth, a 'silo mentality' emerges and people and customers see nothing but frustrating blockages that slow and suffocate the organisation.

When our consulting team receive calls from organisations seeking a solution to these concerns they hear comments such as:

- *turf fights between functions are damaging the customer experience*
- *cost overruns on new initiatives are blowing out the budget*
- *getting a new product to market only happens when a leader rams it through from start to finish*
- *problems are sitting unclaimed in a stand-off between two divisions*
- *change is near impossible because the silos block everything.*

## the silos are not guilty

Not surprisingly, there has been a flood of books and articles encouraging leaders to 'demolish the silos' and replace them with a utopia of engaged people working together in one big community. This reeks of a technical solution to an adaptive problem and, unfortunately, it has encouraged many to try some type of 'destroy the silos' initiative, only to end up with worse performance due to outbreaks of status wars, conflicting priorities and resistance to change.

The core lesson is clear and repeatable: The silos are not guilty!

This is not about organisation structure. There are many examples of enterprises with silo structures that don't suffer from the silo mentality and equally there are plenty that have tried open structures only to be crushed by tribalism and turf protection.

Let's be clear: the 'make or break' is *not* about divisional or matrix structures—it's about the practices and behaviours of alignment, collaboration and learning within and between teams. Put simply, the organisations that perform and adapt well in volatile and competitive environments are brilliant at teamwork across the same types of boundaries that others struggle to breach.

The think one team method reveals the five practices (called 'the five shares') that characterise these organisations.

In a world where every business needs to escape the limitations of silo behaviours the five shares are a simple and proven model and language for engaging and inspiring people to learn and adapt together.

The following section further explains the five shares and how to bring them to life in everything from day-to-day business to organisational transformation. Further details can be found at www.thinkoneteam.com.

# the foundation

From studying and consulting with many different-sized organisations across the business and non-business world, it became clear to me that there were quite distinct differences between the practices of people within silo-afflicted organisations and those of people who acted like one big team.

This experience led to identifying five core practices that distinguish these two types of organisation. Each of these practices has an opposite, or 'shadow'. For example, 'share the big picture' has as its shadow, 'pursue other agendas'.

| think one team | think silos |
|---|---|
| Share the big picture | Pursue other agendas |
| Share the reality | Avoid and deny |
| Share the air | Stifle communication |
| Share the load | Look after your own turf |
| Share the wins and losses | Play 'I win, you lose' |

A brief overview of the five practices, or five shares as they've come to be known, is outlined below.

- *Share the big picture* means that everyone and every team understands and shares their part in the bigger picture. That picture may be of the strategic priorities and values, or simply an understanding of what's happening in the next department. It also includes awareness of the context in which the organisation operates (particularly the threats and opportunities), so that people understand the 'why' behind decisions. The shadow, *pursue other agendas*, is characterised by the individual parts of the organisation pursuing other things that they consider to be more important than the big picture. The reasons for this are usually less about malevolent intentions and more about the 'experts in silos' mentality that many managers still encourage and reinforce.

- *Share the reality* is about getting the truth out on the table, confronting the harsh reality and being open to giving and receiving feedback. The shadow is *avoid and deny*, which is all about protective and defensive behaviours. Its guises include putting an overly positive spin on issues or avoiding them altogether. When reality is avoided or denied the whole organisation is at risk.

- *Share the air* is essential when fast learning and adaptation are needed. Open, two-way communication; engaged listening; and transparency stop the damaging silo mentality from flourishing. However, when the shadow, *stifle communication*, emerges, people dominate others or, alternatively, they hoard information and foster a 'them and us' culture that blocks initiative and agility. Arguably the most important thing a leader can do to engage their team and others is to share the air by encouraging collaboration and co-creation.

- *Share the load* is seen in clear accountability, agreed priorities, collaborating on problems and giving others a helping hand. The shadow, *look after your own turf*, reveals itself as in-company competition, narrow self-interest and hoarding resources and information.

- *Share the wins and losses* reminds us that in big teams everyone wins, loses and learns together. This is the all-important 'closing the loop', which is a feature of high-performing teams. The shadow, *play 'I win, you lose'*, sees people taking credit for wins, while blaming losses on others. This reduces the energy we get from achieving success and the opportunities to learn and get stronger from setbacks.

As you reflect on the five shares in your organisation, notice how when one shadow is allowed to prevail, it begins to affect the others, and when one positive share strengthens, it pulls the others towards it. For example, when people stop sharing the air it won't take long before they start to blame others and just look after their own turf. On the other hand, when people do share the air they develop a much better understanding of how they can support each other—and that leads to shared wins.

Of course, recognising the behaviours is one thing, but the key is to answer the question:

*How do we bring these behaviours and practices to life and make them sustainable?*

The answer to that question took more than three years for our team to finally crack and when we did, it didn't just connect the silos, it also revealed a way of developing the change readiness and resilience that's so essential to handling disruptive change.

That breakthrough provided an essential blueprint for high performance teamwork which is described in detail in the book *toolkit for turbulence* and supplemented with extra tools at www.toolkitforturbulence.com.

The following section explains this breakthrough and how it provides the scaffolding that empowers leaders and teams to address their biggest challenges.

# the learning loop (ACL)

Sometimes the most obvious things are the hardest to see.

That was the case when we were seeking the best way to embed one team tools into the day-to-day operating rhythm of teams and organisations.

From many years of experience working with elite sporting teams I've always been mindful of the simple principle that the last thing learned is the first forgotten under pressure.

This is a great reminder that no matter how effective a training workshop, coaching session or resource guide is, the true test of whether a concept is useful is that it 'sticks' in the day-to-day cut and thrust of business life.

For the coach of a sports team the secret to that 'stickability' is setting up a deliberate, three-step learning and performance loop:

*Step 1:* understand the behaviour (Align)

*Step 2:* practise it as a team under pressure (Collaborate)

*Step 3:* ensure frequent feedback (Learn).

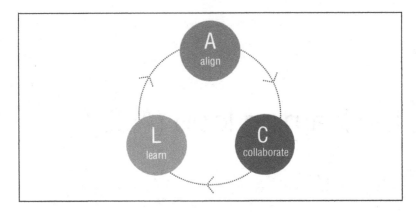

This loop of Align–Collaborate–Learn (ACL) is something that I've seen woven successfully into sports team coaching for two decades; however, the lightbulb went on in two moments of insight.

The first breakthrough was to guide business teams to create a deliberate Align–Collaborate–Learn loop of conversations and practices (in other words, an operating rhythm) to develop good habits around these three elements.

*Align* meant defining the timing and style of meetings and planning for long-term issues such as vision, values and goals; and short-term issues such as priorities, expectations and roles.

*Collaborate* meant deliberately seeking better ways of working together to co-create solutions to problems and opportunities.

*Learn* meant being open to gaining new skills and knowledge and setting aside time to reflect and debrief experiences, and to apply learnings.

Teams that had struggled to get past the short-term benefits of team-building workshops showed immediate benefits from having a disciplined loop of alignment, collaboration and learning. And they kept on improving because the ACL is a natural learning loop that's perfectly suited to adaptive change (that is, learning through issues requires multiple loops of the ACL).

The second lightbulb moment was painfully obvious as we looked at ways of bringing the ACL loop into cross-boundary, team-to-team and colleague-to-colleague partnering. This table shows just how obvious it was.

| align | share the big picture |
|---|---|
| collaborate | share the reality<br>share the air<br>share the load |
| learn | share the wins and losses |

We realised immediately that the way to get behaviours that characterise the five shares to stick in the workplace was to embed the ACL loop into every relationship (formally or informally).

The 'how' behind this was easy because the core tools of 'think one team'—such as Ninety-day Clipboards, problem-solving templates and action debriefing guides—were exactly what people needed to populate the ACL.

Within weeks we had colleagues, teams, divisions and whole organisations shifting from silo-based 'cold war tactics' to actively aligning, collaborating and learning with each other.

Soon these people stopped talking about 'think one team' as a team building program and started referring to it as their 'ways of working'.

Leaders were excited because in ACL they had a way of navigating their team through the challenges of adaptive change. How? Simply by relentlessly spinning the ACL loop to align, collaborate, learn, realign, and so on.

## to recap ...

In summary, the think one team method brings three powerful yet simple insights together:

1   *The big challenges are adaptive (not just technical):* which means that the traditional 'experts in silos' model has to be replaced with collaboration and co-creation across boundaries.

2   *It's not about silos ... it's about five 'shares':* the organisations that successfully collaborate across traditional boundaries typically demonstrate five practices that enable them to be more agile, responsive and effective than organisations that struggle with silo practices.

3   *It's about learning together ... using an ACL loop:* high-performing teams display a dynamic, continuous cycle of three conversations about *Alignment, Collaboration* and *Learning*. This is a natural performance and learning loop that helps teams to adapt to whatever the world throws at them.

Think one team establishes and strengthens this performance and learning loop within and between teams and in partnerships through deliberate practice and carefully targeted tools that reinforce the five shares.

Arguably the most important step in establishing and embedding the one team approach is unity of leadership, which is the next topic we'll address.

# united leadership

*the crucial ingredient in organisation success*

When leaders are united, it creates an environment in which there is clear direction, collaboration, teamwork and leverage of effort. On the other hand, a disjointed group of leaders is almost certain to disengage talented people and cause the organisation to perform well below expectations.

## what united leaders do

United leadership is about leaders at all levels setting a visible example of the five shares in their own actions as individuals and collectively by:

- communicating a sense of purpose and direction (share the big picture)
- creating a feedback environment so people learn and grow (share the reality)
- engaging or involving people to tap the ideas and energy of everyone (share the air)

- collaborating and supporting, while playing their individual parts (share the load)
- seeking success together (share the wins and losses).

You can tell that leaders are united when they put the health of the whole organisation ahead of their own politics or agendas. Questions such as 'What's best for the business?' or 'How can we support you to make that happen?' build confidence and trust that everyone wants everyone else to succeed.

One of the simple tools we use with leadership groups to test the unity is to put people in small groups and ask them to challenge each other to reflect on how strongly they have modelled the ten behaviours in the table below over the past week.

Try the test yourself by seeing how many of the ten you can provide a tangible example of from your past week.

| share the big picture | • instil a strong sense of direction, even in times of uncertainty<br>• connect people to the customer experience |
| --- | --- |
| share the reality | • tackle the tough conversations constructively<br>• seek feedback about your own impact on people |
| share the air | • build trust by listening, enquiring and sharing<br>• create forums and interactions across functions |
| share the load | • give something without expecting anything in return<br>• bring people together to tackle the unclaimed problems |
| share the wins and losses | • facilitate an action debrief to capture learnings<br>• give specific positive reinforcement to a colleague |

## lifting the unity across all leaders

A university that embraced the think one team method over recent years reported five benefits from strengthening the unity among its large leadership cohort, namely:

- stronger alignment on vision, purpose and priorities
- greater openness and trust to have the robust conversations
- confidence in the team structures and frameworks
- faster learning and ability to deliver outcomes
- stronger image of united leadership to others in the organisation.

These are benefits that every organisation would like to achieve and yet when the initiative began the first question we posed to the leaders was:

*What do putting a person on the moon, reaching the summit of Everest and winning an Olympic gold medal all have in common?*

You can imagine the debate among academics! The answer we were seeking was that these are all graphic examples of what are called 'superordinate goals'.

A superordinate goal is a goal that can't be achieved individually but can be achieved collectively. In other words, an individual working alone can't summit Everest, but this can be achieved by a group or team of people who work together towards that common goal.

Superordinate goals have been shown to reduce conflict, and inspire collaboration and exceptional outcomes in many settings around the world.

The university leaders struggled for some time to find a compelling superordinate goal and there were murmurs from some that their time could be better spent researching and teaching in their faculties (being experts in silos!).

Fortunately, one of the newest leaders of the group (with a bit of prompting from the facilitator) chose the perfect moment to question some of the more jaded members as to why they worked at the university and, more particularly, when they had felt most passionate about their work.

This provoked an animated discussion from which emerged one clear and shared belief: that education can transform lives. This was the spark that lit the bonfire and within half an hour more than fifty leaders were united as one in that their superordinate goal was to harness the power of education to transform their own organisation and the community that they served.

Since that moment the unity among leaders has been outstanding. They have embraced the challenges (and squirms) of transformation as one united team and achieved a decade's progress in little more than a year.

Superordinate goals are not always easy to find; however, they inspire people, give meaning, and ultimately create success for the whole team, organisation or system.

Creating a one team culture is in itself a superordinate goal because it can't be achieved by one individual, but it can certainly be achieved by a united group of leaders. Furthermore, when you have united leadership you'll inevitably find more superordinate goals.

Still wondering about your superordinate goal? Remember the proposition at the beginning of the book, 'Imagine the possibilities when everyone in your organisation thinks and acts as one big team'. Imagine superior service, imagine fewer cost overruns on new technology upgrades, imagine more targeted sales campaigns, imagine better talent management, imagine faster commercialisation of new products, imagine anything and chances are you're thinking of a superordinate goal.

As the O'Donnell's story illustrates, the power of working together as one team is sparked by leadership—specifically, united leadership—and that happens in two places.

First is the unity among the executive and divisional leadership teams and second is the unity among leaders of cross-functional teams. Those needs are reflected often in two core ways in which the think one team method is implemented:

- *United Leadership Team Foundation*—which targets the leadership teams and develops the all-important alignment and team dynamics
- *Coaching the Culture*—which equips leaders and advocates to drive their change initiatives through day-to-day activities, collaboration and co-creation.

We will explore a bit of the United Leadership Team approach now and then take a more expansive view of the role of leaders in Coaching the Culture.

## united leadership teams

The most powerful way to begin creating a one-team culture is by building the foundation of alignment, collaboration and learning within leadership teams.

While most people assume this should start with the Executive Team we've found that in medium to larger organisations it's equally, if not more, effective to begin with one of the operational leadership teams (for example, sales, production or logistics).

Senior operations leaders are in an ideal position to open the doors and windows of the silos. Starting with them and running a ninety-day United Leadership Foundation is like preparing the paddock for sewing the crop. It creates a fertile environment for the 'think one team' practices to grow.

It's also fair to say that Executive Teams are unique and subject to many dynamics that don't apply to the divisional teams, so they need very skilled facilitation. This isn't a reason to avoid taking on Executive Teams upfront; it simply means that there are advantages in starting with divisional teams, and there are some challenges to be mindful of when facilitating Executive Teams.

The O'Donnell's Executive Team story illustrates the steps involved in the ninety-day foundation and there are further details in the 'think one team programs' section later in the book, so I won't repeat them here other than to remind you that the key is to establish the operating rhythm and to use tools such as the Ninety-day Clipboard, Collaborative Problem Solving, debriefing and team profile to create and fill the scaffolding.

# coaching the culture
*the new core capability for every leader*

Take a moment to consider this question:

> *Are there any major initiatives in your organisation that*
> *don't require people to collaborate and co-create across the*
> *traditional boundaries between business units, levels of*
> *hierarchy, locations and stakeholders?*

The answer, as is the case in the vast majority of organisations, is almost certainly a resounding 'no'.

One further question:

> *Have any change initiatives underachieved or failed*
> *because silo behaviour has restricted or even prevented the*
> *essential cross-boundary collaboration and teamwork?*

If the answer is 'yes', it's important to take a look at the leadership and change approaches in use and the capability of leaders to coach a culture of one team thinking and behaviours.

At a time when every organisation is continually adapting to shifts in technology, markets and financial demands, silo-based practices must be minimised if people are to successfully collaborate across the traditional boundaries to create solutions and new approaches.

# how to minimise the silo effect

The key to minimising the silo effect is to equip and support the business unit leaders who are at the frontline of driving performance and change across the organisation.

It's ironic that leaders today have probably never had more access to information and tools, but the harsh reality is that they remain ill equipped or unsupported to garner the collaboration that's so essential. There are four reasons for this.

## change has changed

Most business unit leaders are appointed to their roles because of technical competence and skills in solving problems in their areas of expertise. Unfortunately, the big challenges are not just technical in nature, but rather are complex and adaptive, which means that traditional 'within silo' problem solving and linear change management methods don't suit the ambiguity, fast learning and squirming that accompany adaptive change.

## workload + roles = leaders set up to fail

The demands on leaders have never been greater. The combination of flattened or matrix structures and tight budgets makes the leader more of a 'leading hand' than a true team or divisional leader.

The design of work no longer matches the real priorities and leaves leaders drowning in operational workloads, despite the rhetoric that leadership is the highest priority.

## HR is out of date

At a time when leaders need HR to deliver on the promise of learning on the job (70–20–10) and real engagement with employees and stakeholders, many are still hamstrung by performance management systems, employee surveys and training processes that have changed little in decades.

Obsolete HR practices aren't necessarily the fault of practitioners, who are too often undervalued by leaders and not treated as true partners in coaching the culture.

HR has a massive role to play in unlocking the potential of people, teams and organisations. To do this they need to build partnering relationships with leaders and embrace the search for greater productivity, while balancing the requirements for compliance and employee support.

## *collaborative technology doesn't collaborate*

Despite the flood of so-called collaborative technologies, the reality is that many systems are not designed for the shared learning and adaptation that characterises true co-creation.

Team members lack the engagement platforms that are essential for co-creating with people who don't sit in the workspace next to them.

There is a vast range of collaboration tools available but too few teams are using these to support and enhance their align, collaborate, learn operating rhythm. Perhaps one reason is the tendency to expect the technology to do the work, when it is really about good conversations and a disciplined rhythm so the collaboration happens irrespective of busyness and disruption.

# which capabilities and tools are needed?

A new generation of leaders is emerging and they are skilled at Coaching the Culture (CtC).

These CtC leaders display three core sets of capabilities that are easily observed as they connect people, ideas and actions across what others see as almost impenetrable boundaries and barriers.

## *set #1: alignment through ambiguity*

While traditional managers expect business plans and role descriptions to give them alignment with other business units, the CtC leader understands the need to align where a clearly defined goal isn't possible.

Goals change, priorities change, new ideas emerge and business models are discarded. Traditional alignment of goals and plans is too slow.

For the CtC leader, two beliefs and practices stand out.

### relationships trump KPIs

When push comes to shove, the CtC leader knows that alignment of goals and priorities between teams will never be perfect, so they devote time to building partnering relationships with colleagues and stakeholders. And they do this by displaying empathy. This builds the rapport and trust that enables people to live with ambiguity and imperfect alignment.

### operating rhythm is key

The CtC leader recognises the ineffectiveness of annual plans and performance reviews, preferring instead to find the right rhythm or tempo for each situation. That can mean quarterly (not annual) plans, daily debriefs (not end-of-project reviews) and 'fly-past' meetings of five minutes instead of the hourly meeting every Tuesday. For the CtC leader timing is everything, so they don't let old traditions dictate when is the right time to get something done.

## set #2: real engagement

Just about every manager will happily report that they have engaged and are collaborating with their colleagues.

Perhaps this is true, but what do engagement and collaboration really mean?

For the CtC leader, engagement is multifaceted and targeted across four levels:

- *communication* — keeping colleagues informed
- *consultation* — seeking ideas, opinions and perceptions

- *collaboration*—working in sync towards shared or compatible goals
- *co-creation*—total commitment to creating something of value together.

Too many leaders (and organisations) call engagement 'collaboration'when it is in fact consultation at best.

The new leadership capabilities include fostering a shared language, and tools and platforms so that people from diverse backgrounds can find ways to successfully collaborate and co-create.

Co-creation is incredibly powerful and it breaks through the change resistance that so many linear change management methods assume to be inevitable.

## set #3: reflect, learn, adapt

If there's one capability, more than any other, that's lacking across team leaders in industry and government, it's the ability to guide teams and colleagues to reflect and debrief their experiences, and then to use the learnings to improve and adapt.

The CtC leader embeds action debriefing into the operating rhythm to capture insights and new knowledge on the run (while traditional managers schedule the formal debriefing meeting when all is done and dusted).

The new leadership capabilities include facilitating the action debrief, encouraging deep reflection on personal and team behaviours, and translating learning into new business practices.

### urgent message: equip your leaders

Employee engagement is always essential and never more so than when facing significant change.

The onus for engaging staff and leading them through change must sit with the team leader and not with a separate change management function.

It is essential that HR takes the lead here to ensure that leaders are equipped and supported to play this role.

Handing responsibility for managing change to specialists just doesn't make sense when change is continual and adaptive.

A change leadership framework incorporating one team capabilities empowers leaders and gives them the confidence, skills and shared language to make adaptive change a natural feature of every team's activities.

# strengthening team-to-team collaboration

Are you looking for a way to engage your team and colleagues in a conversation about strengthening teamwork and collaboration within and between teams?

The proven way to do this is through a three-step approach:

- *Step 1: introduce the five shares model.* The 'five shares' is the simplest way to introduce a 'one-team conversation' because it creates a practical and tangible framework instead of a general discussion about what 'one team' does or doesn't mean.

    My advice is always to do this using an 'above-the-line/below-the-line' tool format that we call 'Five Shares Quick Wins'. This tool, which is further explained at www.thinkoneteam.com, describes four behaviours or practices for each of the five shares (in other words, what teams do when they successfully collaborate across boundaries) and their opposites (when silo practices prevail). Later in this section we explore these behaviours and there are tips and extra tools to stimulate your conversations and actions.

- *Step 2: identify and prioritise some quick wins.* The specific behaviours and practices for each of the five shares sets up the opportunity to ask the team or group to identify 'quick wins' that can generate business improvement.

  Again, there is a simple way to do this and it was described in the O'Donnell's story when people did the 'Stop, Start, Continue' exercise. In other words, give people the list of behaviours and practices and ask them to define what they might stop, start or continue doing to have an immediate positive impact on the business. Be sure to agree on three or fewer priorities so there is a clear and united focus.

- *Step 3: build momentum.* For most teams, the 'Stop, Start, Continue' conversation generates energy and momentum, while creating familiarity with the think one team method. You can build on this by applying other tips and tools, which are explained in the next section, or make the decision to go straight to defining a ninety-day plan to build team unity or drive a united business change initiative.

Let's explore each of the five shares and some tips and tools for engaging your team and creating that momentum.

## share the big picture

To vividly see what 'share the big picture' means, there's no better time than when organisations or communities are in crisis. Instead of separate agendas, we see the loop of Align – Collaborate – Learn in dynamic action. People share a sense of what's most important; they set aside personal agendas and they learn and adapt fast.

Here are the behaviours and practices in the Five Shares Quick Wins tool. Use them to reflect on your team or wider organisation.

- We share a common purpose.
- We show commitment to an agreed set of values.
- Decisions are made by thinking, 'What's best for the whole?'
- We show respect by considering the impact of our actions on our partners.

**Share the big picture**

**Pursue other agendas**

- We lack understanding of others' respective situations.
- We encourage or allow conflicting agendas to prevail.
- Opportunities are missed because of silo thinking.
- We lack alignment to the big picture.

At a personal level we can all play our part in sharing the big picture by taking a broader perspective on issues, thinking longer term, putting aside local agendas and inviting others to collaborate.

## tips and tools for sharing the big picture

For leaders and teams there's almost a limitless choice of tools and techniques that can be used to help them share the big picture. Let's look at a handful that are particularly useful for developing change readiness and resilience.

### create a compelling story

Stories capture people's imagination, which is why the most effective change leaders create and share a clear, concise and compelling story of the big picture.

Create your own story by using a structure built on the five shares framework as shown in the template below.

| share the big picture | Here is the big picture:<br>• our environment—why change is needed<br>• our purpose, vision and values |
|---|---|
| share the reality | Here are some of the realities that we face in meeting these adaptive challenges:<br>• weaknesses and threats<br>• strengths and opportunities |
| share the air | Why one team is essential:<br>• diversity in ideas and problem solving<br>• trusting each other |
| share the load | How we can share the load:<br>• accountabilities/roles<br>• where partnering is needed |
| share the wins and losses | Our alternative futures:<br>• if we work as one team ...<br>• if we are divided ... |

Use the template as a slide deck initially while drafting the details. Then refine it by using the tests of 'clear, concise and compelling' to ensure you get the understanding and emotional buy-in from your audience.

## connect strategy to team behaviours

Most organisations have a planning (and budgeting) process that cascades mission, vision and values from an overall strategic plan into business unit plans.

From these plans the teams distil their own goals, add a set of ground rules, file all that on the shared drive and then get busy until the next round of business planning!

This process misses the point that direction setting in a dynamic, changeable environment must create the operating tempo of alignment, collaboration and learning that drives performance and learning.

That's why the think one team method combines two tools (the Strategy Diamond and the Ninety-day Clipboard) to connect the longer term direction to the essential short-term team priorities and behaviours.

A Strategy Diamond is anything but rocket science. It's simply a visual tool (used mostly by executive and divisional leadership teams) that gives every employee an unequivocal picture of the driving force or purpose and the top four or five business priorities for the medium to longer term. In the O'Donnell's story the driving force was to 'Create the O'Donnell's experience' and there were four sharp strategic priorities. You will know that you've done it well if in 30 seconds your audience gets it and sees where they can personally contribute.

The second tool is the Ninety-day Clipboard and this is your essential 'align' tool for any and every team. Begin by creating a framework that includes the key inputs to high performance. In the 'think one team' ninety-day initiatives we use the proprietary ADEP model (Achieve – Develop – Enjoy – Partner).

The best way to develop a Ninety-day Clipboard is in a tightly facilitated three-to-four-hour workshop meeting (usually with online preparation and post-session refinement). Start the process by getting your team to answer four core questions:

- What are our top priorities for the next ninety days?
- What do we need to get better at?
- How do we make this enjoyable and sustainable?
- How do we strengthen our most important partnering relationships?

A team with a clear and concise clipboard has the 'scaffolding' that drives operating rhythm, one-team behaviours and performance. Importantly, when this is the norm across multiple teams, you then have the basis for a culture of nimble, connected teams. Devote the time and energy to it: the benefits can be outstanding!

---

**what 'share the big picture' means when implementing change**

▶ keep people aware of the wider context in which they are working (the big picture)

▶ find and connect everything to the driving force or purpose and top priorities

▶ establish the Ninety-day Clipboard habit for every team to drive performance and partnering.

---

## share the reality

If there's a single behaviour or practice that characterises teams and organisations that embrace the think one team method it's the openness to put the difficult issues on the table and debate them constructively. This gives enormous agility and power because instead of avoiding issues or getting embroiled in ego-based conflict, the teams address the 'elephants' and move on.

Here are the behaviours and practices in the Five Shares Quick Wins tool.

- People feel free to speak the truth respectfully and openly.
- We give and receive useful feedback.
- We deliver what we each need and expect.
- We debate and make decisions based on evidence or data.

**Share the reality**

**Avoid and deny**

- There is a lot of spin on information.
- People avoid direct, honest feedback conversations.
- The tough conversations or issues are usually avoided.
- Reality checks are avoided.

In a high-performing team there's no topic that can't be raised and discussed in an open and constructive manner. At a personal level you can encourage this culture of openness by inviting people to challenge and provide feedback on your own behaviours and performance. This sets the tone and encourages everyone to have the courage and composure to calmly put a controversial issue on the table.

## tips and tools for sharing the reality

In the absence of trust it's very difficult to create the openness to challenge and be challenged. For that reason it's important to find ways of reducing the need for people to protect or defend themselves.

Here are three ideas that have been successful across many different organisations.

### go one-on-one to build rapport and empathy

One of the simplest and most useful tools in the 'think one team' suite is colleague-to-colleague partnering, which provides two colleagues with the framework to have a conversation with each other that sets the basis for a partnering relationship. This tool encourages people to make time for quality one-on-one dialogue that builds rapport and empathy with staff, colleagues and other stakeholders.

In a busy workplace, it's difficult to prioritise the 'coffee catch-up' conversations; however, time and again we find people reflecting at the end of a ninety-day initiative on how beneficial it was to build these relationships. When asked why, they usually explain that it's easier to share the reality, which resulted in breaking through bottlenecks and reducing conflicts that previously disrupted the business.

### make feedback a way of life

Inviting, accepting and offering feedback is one of the most powerful ways of building trust while also gaining greater self-awareness.

One approach that we use extensively to develop feedback skills and confidence is called Feedback Circles. These are structured group activities woven into business meetings and training workshops, in which people seek and receive verbal insights and feedback from their colleagues. These Feedback Circles have tightly defined ground rules and can range from conversations where people only offer positive insights (reinforcing strengths) through to much more challenging situations where every team member receives improvement feedback from every other team member.

The key to the success of any feedback activity is the role modelling by the team leader and senior members because their attitude to feedback either encourages others to be open and constructive, or it closes them down.

Many people have found a simple tool called the 3Rs to be very helpful as a 'how to' guide for receiving their feedback in an emotionally intelligent way. The basics of this tool are shown in this table.

| receive | • be open in your voice and body language<br>• actively listen<br>• say 'thanks, I appreciate your thoughts' |
|---------|---|
| reflect | • think about the message<br>• separate the emotion from the detail<br>• choose your response |
| respond | • seek more understanding<br>• make changes as required<br>• ask for more feedback |

## act like a (friendly) venture capitalist

If you had just five minutes to make a business-critical decision on whether a new initiative should be launched or not, which questions would you ask and what data would you want?

In the normal corporate world, of course, you would have a lot more time, and no doubt plenty of data to assist with the decision. Perhaps. Or maybe you're working in a fast-moving culture of nimble, connected teams, where you would receive a short, sharp report highlighting just three things: Assumptions, Risk and Return.

If you want to speed up your team and get more 'share the reality conversations', then ask anyone who presents a business case to answer three sets of questions:

- What are the key assumptions that you have made?
  And how can we test those assumptions with minimal investment of time, money, effort and other resources?

- What are the most important risks? And what is their likelihood and impact?

- What is the return on investment? And how do you rate your confidence in this happening?

A venture capitalist would eliminate many options based on these three sets of questions, so why not do the same?

When facing complex, ambiguous decisions it makes sense to draw out the assumptions and find ways to test them without investing too much. In start-up businesses this is called a Minimum Viable Product (MVP), and when combined with a good awareness of risk and return it delivers better results than traditional management approaches.

---

**what 'share the reality' means when implementing change**

▶ openness and feedback are your friends

▶ there are no sacred cows — everything is open to being challenged

▶ state and test the assumptions, then decide based on risk and return.

---

## share the air

The power of 'one team' comes from tapping the diversity of ideas, energy and intelligence across the organisation or community. That means opening up the lines of communication and encouraging people to co-create solutions to problems and opportunities.

The opposite of sharing the air is stifling communication and it has two sides to it.

First is controlling or dominating the conversations, which restricts input and leads to poor decisions with even poorer buy-in from the people who are expected to implement them.

Second is 'spectating' rather than initiating and participating constructively in discussions. The reasons for this are many, ranging from lack of suitable collaboration forums and platforms, through to personal style and hoarding information.

Here are the behaviours and practices in the Five Shares Quick Wins tool.

- Communication between us is open and constructive.
- We follow a disciplined communication plan.
- We make a concerted effort to build trust.
- Our meetings and forums are productive.

**Share the air**

**Stifle communication**

- Alternative views get dismissed or criticised.
- People or functions dominate cross-business meetings.
- There is too much 'turf protection' of information and power.
- We are too guarded, which inhibits trust.

## tips and tools for sharing the air

The essence of sharing the air is to encourage the flow of ideas, opinions and information through the organisation. At a personal level we can all help to share the air by asking for others' help and opinions, by being available and cooperative, and by listening attentively.

This plays a vital role in connecting the silos through better relationships and alignment.

Here are some key ways to share the air.

### encourage team-to-team partnering

Most organisations spend a good deal of time and effort on team building for business units but little on connecting those teams. In many ways this is ironic because it's the cross-boundary linkages that are most at risk of unclear purpose, differing expectations (implicit or explicit) and incompatible cultural styles.

That's why there are so many unclaimed benefits to be found by establishing partnering relationships and agreements between teams. Apart from the obvious upsides of greater productivity and performance, these include:

- better alignment and leveraging of resources
- faster learning and adaptation
- less operational and reputational risk
- improved engagement of employees.

If you'd like to see these potential benefits in your organisation then look for ways to bring teams together to build rapport, to align expectations and to establish the ACL loop.

The think one team method includes a team-to-team partnering ninety-day program that's popular among alliances and large organisations. Three critical success factors in these programs are to:

- first, take time to build empathy between teams
- second, establish clear expectations about outcomes and behaviours
- third, include a regular process of debriefing and learning.

When the expectations and debriefing are defined in a partnering agreement (with an operating rhythm) it minimises the divisiveness that often arises from natural tensions between teams.

## engage early and often

It's essential to have a variety of engagement and collaboration platforms to encourage and enable people to share the air. These range from meetings, forums and workshops to online collaboration platforms and other social and business media.

Take time to reflect on the people with whom you want your team to engage and then ask if they have the right platforms for engaging early and often as change unfolds. Too often this is left to chance and people end up with a choice between email or poorly designed meetings and forums.

## go beyond active listening

Have you ever been to a course on listening skills? Even if you haven't, you'll be familiar with the concept of active listening.

A typical course will train you to do something that fits perfectly with the acronym AIR:

- **Attend** — give the person your full attention
- **Inquire** — ask open questions
- **Reflect** — show understanding through summarising.

Unfortunately, that's not quite enough because I find that the customs officers at international airports demonstrate these three behaviours but I don't get the sense that they want to share the AIR!

What's missing?

In a word, 'engagement'.

The customs officer is listening to get the information they want. They aren't trying to engage me in a relationship. And, ironically, I'll be more guarded as a consequence.

Would your colleagues say that you listen, actively listen or really listen to engage them?

167

### call the cynicism

Few things are more damaging to sharing the air than people who take pride in showing their cynicism through their verbal and non-verbal behaviour. Most typical are the people who never say outright that they disagree, but their voice tone, facial expressions and body language all exude an energy-sapping cynicism. This behaviour must be 'called' by members of the team by initially bringing it to the other person's attention. This might be done in an empathic way by saying, 'I'm not sure how things feel from your position, but from mine I'm receiving the message that you're not supportive about what we're doing'.

---

**what 'share the air' means when implementing change**

▶ tapping the collective intelligence — fostering a culture of co-creation

▶ creating platforms so that people engage early and often

▶ bringing teams together to work as partners

▶ calling the cynicism — reinforce engaged listening.

---

# share the load

Sharing the load is where the work gets done and, arguably, it's the 'biggest' of the practices because it reminds us about the big picture and the many roles and tasks that are leading towards it.

Sharing the load means understanding what the load actually is and collaborating when needed to get it done efficiently and effectively.

The opposite of sharing the load is looking after your own turf. This is a common practice in business, partly because most organisations are actually designed (including the reward system)

to encourage people to play to their own or their local team's agendas. 'Acts of teamwork' are needed on many levels to show why sharing the load is a better way to do business.

All too often teams mistake loyalty to their department or division for strong teamwork, while they unwittingly damage the overall organisation to achieve their own ends. This is easily justified with 'I'm just doing my job'; however, it's poison for teamwork across boundaries.

Here are the behaviours and practices in the Five Shares Quick Wins tool.

- We regularly plan and prioritise together.
- We treat each other as equal partners.
- We collaborate successfully on problems and opportunities.
- Our roles and expectations are clear and aligned.

**Share the load**

**Look after your own turf**

- We treat each other as competitors.
- Planning and prioritising mostly happens in isolation.
- Processes and systems cause friction and reduced effectiveness.
- We have inconsistencies in language and practices.

## tips and tools for sharing the load

At a personal level, sharing the load means taking accountability for our roles and for engaging our colleagues. That means being willing to share the load on problems, to challenge and support each other, and to share resources when needed.

### joint planning and prioritisation

To reduce the angst that comes from people looking after their own turf it's important to get them together early in the planning process and to prioritise jointly.

It's the culture in many organisations that people protect their own patch until they finalise their plans, and not surprisingly this creates mayhem for everyone else down the line when they get blindsided. You see it between Manufacturing and Sales, between head office and regions, and between Information Technology and Business Units. It happens everywhere and it's dumb, so don't do it.

### one person accountable, multiple people responsible

This simple mantra can have a dramatic effect across large organisations when the leaders embrace it as a way of aligning, collaborating and learning.

The focus on 'one person accountable' may sound like the opposite of one-team behaviours, but the accountability and responsibility has three pieces to it: it's accountability for the outcome, responsibility for engaging colleagues and stakeholders, and supporting colleagues in their areas of accountability.

These three elements enable teams to move multiple tasks forward quickly, to align on the run and to be ready to implement as a team.

To make it work in your team, ask people to demonstrate that they have engaged their colleagues and have been available to be engaged.

### *look left, look right (take off the blinkers)*

When people understand what's happening around them they're in a much better position to know how they're affecting other people's performance. 'Look left, look right' means spending time outside of your business area, so you (and they) can learn how things have an impact on each other. When combined with training or coaching in emotional intelligence a 'look left, look right' campaign can have a huge positive impact on freeing up the flow of work through an organisation.

---

**what 'share the load' means when implementing change**

▶ bringing people together early to align goals, priorities and roles

▶ moving fast with 'one person accountable, multiple people responsible'

▶ giving people visibility of what's happening in other areas of the business.

---

## share the wins and losses

Everyone shares the wins and the losses in an effective team, which at the most basic level means that they know the score. This is important because in siloed organisations the score tends to be very local (related to just one department), rather than being across-the-silo scores such as speed to market, customer satisfaction or employee engagement.

The opposite of *share the wins and losses* is *play 'I win, you lose'*. People with this mindset think that provided their area of the business is okay, that's just fine by them. They can be found smugly noting that the Sales division is under target or a project team is struggling while they have their department running to budget. Of course, as soon as things change, they will be the first to apportion blame to anyone from management to the courier company, just as long as the blame is not on them.

Another version of this is not focusing on results at all because they convince themselves that it's the process they follow that's most important. From teachers to maintenance workers, and engineers to team leaders, people rationalise processes but lose sight of the need to deliver results.

Here are the behaviours and practices in the Five Shares Quick Wins tool.

- Close attention is paid to performance and results.
- We debrief and share learning.
- We celebrate wins.
- We succeed because of great collaboration.

**Share the wins and losses**

**Play 'I win, you lose'**

- People look to blame when things go wrong.
- Disciplined and intensive debriefing rarely happens.
- Process is more important than outcomes.
- We are struggling because we don't share the wins and losses.

A key to sharing the wins and losses is the learning that comes from success and setback. We can all encourage this by celebrating our successes and reinforcing strengths while relentlessly capturing the lessons learned from the more difficult times.

## tips and tools for sharing the wins and losses

The most important step is to ensure that there are clear goals and scoreboards so that everyone understands and can see progress. This has been a key feature of production lines for years as companies realised that people perform better when they're accountable for the whole result rather than just a small section.

### instil the operating rhythm

The notion of operating rhythm or tempo is fundamental to creating a team that performs, learns and adapts in volatile and challenging conditions.

While the Align–Collaborate–Learn loop usually begins with alignment, it's often the process of reflecting on the wins and losses that closes the loop and generates the next cycle of realignment and collaboration.

In a changeable environment there are few more important roles for team leaders than instilling the ACL loop and ensuring that the drumbeat is fast and regular.

### celebrate within and across the boundaries

Teams and departments are rarely good at celebrating their own successes, which means that getting two or more together to do it is quite a challenge. The good news is that bringing people together to share the wins (such as winning a deal or launching a new product) almost always has an immediate positive impact because it's so unexpected. Why not invite a few people to celebrate a recent achievement?

## *close the loop: debrief relentlessly*

The use of action debriefing—with a focus on learning and adapting—is a great way of getting people to share the reality and to be personally connected to the wins and losses.

An action debrief is a discussion about an event or period of activity, focused on performance standards, that enables people to reflect on what happened, why it happened, and how to sustain strengths and improve on weaknesses.

The key words are 'performance standards' because it's those standards that provide the framework for the team discussion. Not surprisingly, the nimble teamwork in many non-business settings such as special military, emergency medicine and Olympic sport is underpinned by a culture of relentless and intensive debriefing.

The think one team method embeds the habit of action debriefing into the operating rhythm of teams and partnerships. To introduce this into your team, just choose an event or activity and facilitate a conversation using these four questions:

- What was supposed to happen?

- What did actually happen?

- What were the differences between expectations and reality?

- How can we learn and improve?

These simple questions will produce some lessons learnt. Your task is then to convert them into lessons applied by agreeing to actions and the timing of the next action debrief.

---

**what 'share the wins and losses' means when implementing change**

▶ instil the drumbeat of align, collaborate and learn

▶ recognise and reinforce successes and strengths

▶ close the loop: relentlessly debrief, learn and adapt

▶ turn lessons learnt into lessons applied.

---

# think one team programs

The think one team method and programs have been implemented in hundreds of organisations and are proven to provide rapid and substantial improvements in cross-boundary collaboration and adaptability through the disarmingly simple methodology and 'sticky' set of tools and practices.

Each program is delivered using a blended learning model over a minimum of ninety days using a three-step—warm-up, workshop, workout—method. See www.thinkoneteam.com for further details.

At the time of writing, the majority of think one team programs address three primary needs—united leadership, cohesive teamwork and one team culture.

The style and simplicity of think one team means that the method is attractive for leadership and business teams, and transformation project teams, as well as an enterprise-wide approach to change leadership and change readiness.

# three foundation programs

The three foundation think one team programs are:

- *United Leadership Team Foundation.* This enhances the unity of executive, divisional and business unit teams

- *Cohesive Teams.* This guides teams to form, accelerate their development and sustain performance in volatile and challenging conditions.

- *One Team Culture.* This is about fostering a culture where people openly collaborate and co-create solutions across the boundaries of hierarchy, function and location.

## *united leadership team foundation*

United leadership is one of the most crucial ingredients in any organisation's business and transformation strategy.

United leadership teams create an environment of clearer direction, collaboration, teamwork and leverage for effort.

The United Leadership Team Foundation program is an initiative that lifts the impact of leadership teams by boosting alignment, collaboration and shared learning.

The key focus is on openness and trust through establishing a cycle and style of conversations that build leader-to-leader relationships. During this process the team creates a shared framework to guide and assess team performance and development.

Leadership teams across a wide range of organisations and industries have completed the United Leadership Team Foundation program and report benefits including:

- stronger alignment on vision, purpose and priorities

- greater openness and trust to have the robust conversations

- confidence in the team structures and frameworks

- faster learning and ability to adapt

- stronger image of united leadership to others in the organisation.

## *cohesive teams*

When teams at all levels truly work as one, they display four characteristics:

- Unity — the team is united around what matters and collaborates outside of formal meetings
- Diversity — people with diverse skills, styles and experiences tackle the business challenges together
- Trust — the team leader treats everyone in the team as a partner, and people treat each other as partners
- Adaptability — the team is nimble and adapts quickly to opportunities and threats.

The think one team approach to team building is to bring simple, engaging tools to coach and facilitate team development over a ninety-to-120 day period.

At the outset a team canvas (see www.thinkoneteam.com for details) is used as a blueprint to generate commitment and focus on the areas of greatest impact for team development.

The shared language, practices and one team tools such as collaborative problem solving and debriefing reinforce one team behaviours by strengthening the team dynamics while creating a positive business impact at the same time.

## *one team culture*

The vast majority of enterprises can't successfully adapt and perform unless people collaborate and co-create across the traditional boundaries of business units, hierarchy, location and alliances.

Silo behaviour remains a major impediment to this and current approaches to change management, team building and collaborative technology have had limited impact.

Think one team has shown rapid and significant improvements in cross-boundary collaboration and adaptability through the One Team Culture approach, which provides an easy-to-implement methodology and practical set of tools and practices targeted at the leaders and teams involved in business change and transformation.

During ninety-day cycles of action learning, a team of leaders and advocates apply think one team methods and tools to selected business initiatives. This approach develops internal capabilities, habits and toolkits for leading collaborative change while delivering business results at the same time.

The One Team Culture approach has been applied across a wide range of organisations and has consistently delivered benefits, including:

- stronger alignment and engagement within and between teams
- better and faster solutions to cross-boundary problems
- improved agility and adaptability
- reduced resistance to and fatigue from disruptive change.

## core capability learning packages

A range of think one team learning packages are delivered in blended learning form to support the foundation programs and to meet the demands from leaders and teams for practical methods and tools to strengthen teamwork, collaboration and change readiness.

These learning packages include the following.

### *performance partnering*

Nimble, adaptive and high-performing organisations need better ways to engage their people than the traditional performance management methods. Performance partnering embeds a simple cycle of time-efficient conversations between leaders and employees to create alignment, collaboration and performance improvement. This provides the tools, skills and confidence for people at all levels to hold performance-enhancing conversations.

### *team true north*

Teams perform at their best when there is confidence in and commitment to a shared purpose and way of operating. Team True North helps business unit teams to develop a high-performance framework to guide the team through periods of high pressure, conflicting demands and ambiguity.

### *collaborative problem solving*

The traditional idea that problems are solved by 'experts in silos' just doesn't suit the complex and connected business world of today. The Collaborative Problem Solving learning package builds and reinforces the all-important collaboration skills by instilling a shared language, tools and commitment to tackle problems together.

### *team-to-team partnering*

The difference between success and failure of whole organisations is often the quality of collaboration across the silos. The Team-to-Team Partnering learning package addresses this mission-critical business need by providing teams with a framework, toolkit and guidance to establish strong, sustainable and effective partnering relationships with other teams and stakeholders.

## what's different?

There are three attributes of the think one team method that make it distinctive and popular as an alternative to the traditional leadership, teamwork and change management approaches:

- *Simple, effective models.* The 'five shares' and 'ACL' models are easy to implement from the executive to frontline and provide consistency in leadership, teamwork, performance and change practices across the organisation.

- *Easy-to-apply tools.* There are over one hundred different tools that are used by our facilitators to help leaders and teams make teamwork and collaboration a real strength. These tools are simple, proven and easy to implement in fast changing and high demand environments.

- *Blended learning.* Time-effective training development on action learning, delivered face-to-face and online, instils concepts quickly and easily, while getting behavioural change to stick.

## why 'think one team'?

In a complex, ever-changing world it's hard to imagine a more powerful business strategy than to equip, engage and inspire people to think and act as one team.

That's why so many organisations have chosen think one team to deliver the improvements in teamwork across boundaries, which has led to cost savings, faster new-product commercialisation, leaner business processes, reduced silos, better partnering and a host of other benefits.

Think one team has been successfully implemented in Australia, North and South America, Asia and Europe for whole organisations as well as specific groups, including leadership and management teams, alliances and partnerships, and all manner of cross-functional teams.

I encourage you to imagine the possibilities for your business. For further information about think one team and the associated services, visit www.thinkoneteam.com.

# summary

It's self-evident that organisations can't succeed in a complex, ever-changing world unless people work together.

But what does 'work together' really mean?

I believe it means working as one team. And that means the leaders are united and collaborating as partners, teams are high performing and connected, employees are engaged and productive, and as a consequence the whole organisation is nimble, resilient and change ready.

Of course, that's not the norm across industry and government. Instead of engaged and agile teams that work as one to quickly pursue opportunities and resolve problems, we see costly overruns, service slip-ups, turf fights and duplication.

While many people look to organisation structure and blame the silos, they miss the five distinct practices that differentiate the organisation that works as one from the all-too-familiar opposite.

In a one-team organisation people share a bigger picture than their own business unit agendas; they share the reality by getting the tough issues out on the table and they tap the collective intelligence by sharing the air. They share the load by co-creating solutions to problems and opportunities, and they learn and adapt by sharing the wins and losses.

Every day these one-team organisations can be seen aligning their goals, their expectations and their priorities; collaborating across the same boundaries that shackle others; and relentlessly reflecting, debriefing and learning from their experiences.

It's these organisations that have inspired the creation of the think one team method because this isn't a management theory or a change management checklist—it's a practical guide and toolkit that draws from the real world of business challenges and change.

In your organisation and beyond lie countless emerging challenges that can't be solved within the old ways of silo thinking and technical change management.

The opportunities are endless and there has never been a better time to engage and inspire your team and colleagues to imagine the possibilities when everyone thinks and acts as one big team.

# sample chapter: *toolkit for turbulence*

If this book has engaged and inspired you to bring the power and simplicity of 'think one team' to your organisation, then *toolkit for turbulence* might be just what you need to take things to a whole new level.

Do you want to turn the adversity of disruption into an opportunity to grow and to be a better leader?

Are you always thinking about how to equip, develop and support your team to be the best they can be?

Is performance and wellbeing important to you?

If the answer is 'yes' to any of these questions, then your next step is *toolkit for turbulence*.

Designed around a combination of real-life stories, working models (many derived from *think one team*) and practical tools featuring contributions from top Australian and international business leaders, this is a go to resource for leaders at every level.

The book is co-authored with Martin Bean CBE, who provided the foreword for this book, and structured into six parts beginning with the pathway chosen by successful leaders to navigate from disruption to advantage, then deep diving into three exciting concepts:

- calibrating mindset to excel in volatile and uncertain conditions
- building and sustaining team performance in fast changing conditions
- being the coach your people need to unlock potential.

Woven throughout is the theme, 'Don't just survive adversity, turn it to your advantage'.

*Toolkit for turbulence* is entertaining and thought-provoking, so here's a chapter to whet your appetite. It's called *A Blueprint for Teamwork* and you'll find it starts on familiar ground with the ACL model and then shows you how to use a team canvas to create a blueprint for evaluating, envisioning and sustaining high performance teamwork. I hope you enjoy this chapter, and it inspires you to take the leap to build your own toolkit for turbulence!

# A blueprint for teamwork

*Do you view your team as one of your greatest assets? Are you keen to unlock the potential of your team as individuals and collectively? Is a high-performing team essential to your business strategy and personal aspirations?*

If you've answered 'yes' to any of these questions, then these chapters are for you! They offer a step-by-step guide to transforming team culture and ways of working to suit the challenges of today and tomorrow. You will find chapters chockful of proven tools and techniques to supercharge your team to sustain performance and wellbeing in high-demand conditions.

## A shared framework

The starting point for building a top team is a shared understanding of the essential characteristics or building blocks for a high-performing team. You need that so everyone is clear and aligned about what a top-performing team really is. The challenge is to make it compellingly practical, while not oversimplifying the complexities of team direction, dynamics and development.

In this part we offer a framework to describe, create and evaluate the way your team, or any team, is set up and how it operates. That framework is in the form of a learning loop model that has been applied and proven as part of the Think One Team method (www.thinkoneteam.com) in a wide array of enterprises and government settings ranging from start-ups to the executive teams of multinational corporations. It has also been used to support agile implementations, to fast-track the development of cross-functional tiger teams and to guide the forming, building, and reimagining of countless departmental and divisional teams.

The framework gives you a simple shared language to collaborate with your team and other leadership colleagues to create the optimal operating rhythm, tools and practices. It also provides a baseline for assumptions to be continually challenged and refined — something that is increasingly important in turbulence.

Without a framework, teamwork can be a mystery, or a jumble of important but disconnected ideas like trust, purpose, dynamics and collaboration.

# Three core elements

Observe any team operating effectively at pace in a high-demand environment and at the heart of their ability to deliver consistent high performance will be a loop of three core activities: *Alignment, Collaboration* and *Learning*.

You can use these three elements, called ACL, to shape your team framework and identify the building blocks for any team. When unpacked the team framework offers a blueprint to guide the conversations about team plans, processes and practices. Here are those elements and a powerful set of associated questions.

## Align

To be aligned is to commit to shared direction and focus.

» What is our purpose and vision for success?

» What are our goals and priorities?

» What values and behaviours are important to guide our actions?

Without a shared understanding and commitment to these elements, team members lack unity, engagement and the will to collaborate and learn.

## *Collaborate*

To collaborate is to share in a spirit of working as one.

» How strong is our trust and commitment to each other?

» Are we leveraging resources by co-creating and tackling problems together?

» Is our decision making and execution coordinated?

Without sharing there is inevitably waste, missed opportunities, disengagement, and the risks that come from silos and poorly executed strategies.

## *Learn*

To learn is to be open, agile and adaptable (for a purpose).

» Are we open to learn from feedback, being challenged and reflection?

» Are we empowered, accountable and adding value?

» What's our optimal operating rhythm?

Without adaptability built into your operating rhythm the team will be too slow to respond in the face of rapid and unpredictable change.

## Operating rhythm

While the ACL elements can be described separately, the secret to success is to understand how they interact with one another to create cycles of alignment, collaboration and learning (see figure 10.1).

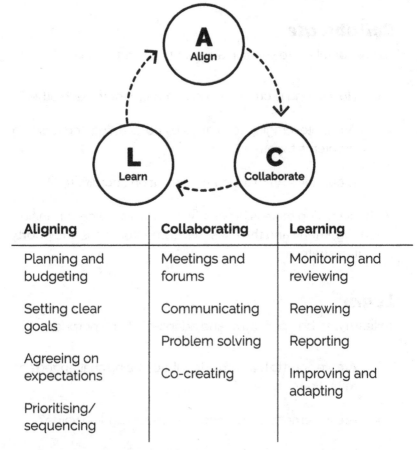

| Aligning | Collaborating | Learning |
| --- | --- | --- |
| Planning and budgeting | Meetings and forums | Monitoring and reviewing |
| Setting clear goals | Communicating | Renewing |
| | Problem solving | Reporting |
| Agreeing on expectations | Co-creating | Improving and adapting |
| Prioritising/ sequencing | | |

**Figure 10.1:** the ACL model

Operating rhythm is the pace and tempo of the rituals, routines and actions by which teams align, collaborate and learn. There is no right or wrong way, just the underlying principle of 'loop and learn' to navigate through changing context, in much the same way as a sailboat skipper and crew continually align, collaborate and learn.

Sometimes the operating rhythm is dictated by the context in which the team is operating. A basketball team has a game-day rhythm; an executive team reports in governance cycles. At other times the team defines its own tempo, such as weekly agile sprints or a 90-day performance cycle.

Paul Duldig reflects on the 90-day or quarterly operating rhythm at Australian National University. 'It has served us really well in crisis and as a way to get the tempo needed to deliver in more settled times. Teams set up and then it's quarterly targets and feedback around the right conversations.'

You'll find more detail and additional tools to help you develop your operating rhythm tempo, principles and practices in chapter 13. For now, just keep in mind that every tool interacts with every other tool in some way. The primary tool *Team Canvas* will show you how to pull them all together for your team.

# Team Canvas

The basic Team Canvas illustrates the three core elements, *align, collaborate* and *learn*, then describes two essential building blocks for team effectiveness in each: *Direction and Focus, Connection and Synergy, Awareness and Tempo*.

Let's explore the tool.

# Team Canvas

The Team Canvas provides the overall framework to evaluate the team setup and choose the optimal tools to sustain and grow team effectiveness.

---

### OVERVIEW

The Team Canvas is your one-page guide to the key building blocks of high-performance teamwork.

You can evaluate your team's current strengths and needs for improvement against the elements on the Team Canvas. The following three chapters provide the tools needed to set up your team to align, collaborate and learn.

# Team Canvas

## (A) Align

### 1 Direction

Clear and meaningful team purpose

Average:

Compelling vision and narrative to capture the hearts and minds of our people

Average:

### 2 Focus

Shared values/principles reflected in team member behaviours

Average:

Agreed priorities and goals for the right horizons

Average:

## (C) Collaborate

### 3 Connection

Healthy interpersonal trust amongst team members

Average:

Strong partnering relationships and practices

Average:

### 4 Synergy

Effective collaborative problem solving and co-creation

Average:

Synergistic decision making

Average:

## (L) Learn

### 5 Awareness

Openness to reflect, give and receive feedback and to challenge

Average:

Relentless debriefing

Average:

### 6 Tempo

Disciplined operating rhythm/ performance cycle cadence

Average:

Delivering outcomes at pace through empowerment and accountability

Average:

# How to use the Team Canvas

To fully set up your team we recommend a process covering five phases: *Evaluate, Envision, Assemble, Implement* and *Adapt*. Figure 10.2 summarises the aims of each phase.

| | |
|---|---|
| **Evaluate** | Identify and quantify your team strengths and gaps. |
| **Envision** | Describe your optimal team setup and ways of working. |
| **Assemble** | Prioritise your team development needs and tools. |
| **Implement** | Weave tools and practices into your team operating rhythm. |
| **Adapt** | Adapt and modify the team practices in response to what's happening. |

**Figure 10.2:** phases in deploying the Team Canvas

The progression through these phases isn't intended to be linear. Assembling and Implementation will likely be continuous while you Evaluate, Envision and Adapt.

For the best results we recommend starting with *Evaluate* and working through this phase personally and with your team.

We'll show how to use the Team Canvas to evaluate and set up the ways of working for your team. The following chapters then deep dive into *Align, Collaborate* and *Learn* to provide the tools you'll need to equip your team to navigate disruption and turn turbulence to advantage.

# *Phase 1. Evaluate*

The aim of this phase is to identify and quantify team strengths and gaps so you can define development priorities for your team and affirm ways of working.

Here we describe an example of how the Team Canvas is used by a team. You can use the same process to conduct your own evaluation.

## CASE EXAMPLE

A team from a human services enterprise used the Team Canvas to evaluate team strengths and gaps for the purpose of setting up for a new year.

Posted on the wall on their arrival was an A0-sized poster of the Team Canvas together with stacks of Post-it notes and sharpies. The facilitator explained how the Team Canvas framework was based on the ACL loop and pointed to the six building blocks, encouraging questions along the way.

The team worked through the canvas one building block at a time. Using a rating scale from –5 (significant derailer) to +5 (significant enabler), each individual was asked to rate the team against the two prompting items by placing Post-it notes with their rating in the appropriate spots.

The facilitator then used a large Post-it to show the average score for each item in that block (see example in figure 10.3, overleaf).

A brief discussion then followed to draw out reasons for the ratings in that block. The facilitator recorded those insights.

**Team Canvas**

Average scores on evaluation

**(A) Align**

**(C) Collaborate**

**(L) Learn**

**1 Direction**

Clear and meaningful team purpose

Average: **+2**

Compelling vision and narrative to capture the hearts and minds of our people

Average: **-1**

**2 Focus**

Shared values/principles reflected in team member behaviours

Average: **+3**

Agreed priorities and goals for the right horizons

Average: **-1**

**3 Connection**

Healthy interpersonal trust amongst team members

Average: **+2**

Strong partnering relationships and practices

Average: **-1**

**4 Synergy**

Effective collaborative problem solving and co-creation

Average: **+3**

Synergistic decision making

Average: **+4**

**5 Awareness**

Openness to reflect, give and receive feedback and to challenge

Average: **+3**

Relentless debriefing

Average: **+2**

**6 Tempo**

Disciplined operating rhythm/performance cycle cadence

Average: **-1**

Delivering outcomes at pace through empowerment and accountability

Average: **+4**

**Figure 10.3:** Team Canvas evaluation

Over approximately 45 minutes the team rated and discussed each item until the Team Canvas provided a clear one-page view of the current maturity of the team in every area of the canvas.

The outcome of this activity was confirmation of three immediate priorities:

1. **Focus**. Define and align on priorities in 90-day cycles.

2. **Connection**. Strengthen partnering relationships and practices among team members.

3. **Tempo**. Tighten the operating rhythm to get greater visibility when things are off track.

Apart from providing a clear sense of strengths and gaps, the Team Canvas evaluation is also an excellent team development activity because it encourages everyone to contribute equally and agree a shared path forward.

One important point to emphasise is that getting a +5 is quite an achievement and it is not expected that teams will want to reach that level on every item. For example, an average score of +3 for 'Clear and meaningful team purpose' could be quite adequate, whereas the team might aim closer to +5 on 'Healthy interpersonal trust'.

## *Phase 2. Envision*

The aim of this phase is to describe the optimal team setup and ways of working. This can be beneficial particularly for new teams or consistency across multiple teams.

The process is straightforward and requires asking the team to debate and define what success will mean for each building block on the canvas. Once complete, it gives a clear framework for choosing tools, prioritising development activities and guiding overall team development.

For example, a defence enterprise has used the canvas for this purpose over several years to shape the development of team capabilities across the whole enterprise.

Figure 10.4 (overleaf) highlights some of the intentions they defined:

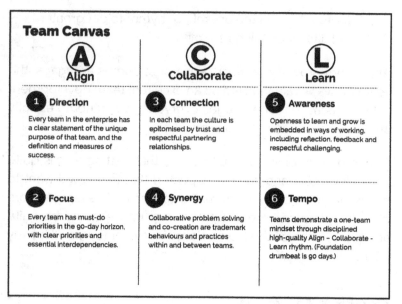

**Figure 10.4:** example of optimal setup for a team of teams

## Phase 3. Assemble

This is the phase where you prioritise development needs and tools based on the insights gained from the earlier phases.

Those tools might be drawn from this book, your own playbooks or other sources. It is up to you to choose those that are most suited to your context and needs.

For example, to *align* your team you might choose to use a *Team Diamond* which is described in the next chapter. This is a great way to efficiently build commitment to the team purpose and high-level priorities.

If the need is to *collaborate*, you might choose to engage everyone in a shared tool like the *PROBED collaborative problem solving* tool in chapter 12.

When your mind turns to *learn*, debriefing tools are covered in chapter 13. You may choose to use them immediately or refine further to build them into your team operating rhythm.

## *Phase 4. Implement*

Implementing your chosen tools and practices is about creating new habits that are integrated into the operating rhythm so they become an ongoing feature of your team's ways of working.

Why integrate them into the operating rhythm? Because they won't stick without discipline. As renowned surgeon Atul Gawande advises about people and their habits, 'We are not built for discipline. We are built for novelty and excitement, not for careful attention to detail. Discipline is something we have to work at.'

Gawande's disciplined use of simple checklists built into operating rhythm transformed the rates of cross-infection in surgery across the world, and his methods have been widely adopted to help professionals to work in disciplined and effective ways.

## *Phase 5. Adapt*

An effective operating rhythm will ensure that you regularly monitor, evaluate and adapt your tools and practices based on what is happening to your team and enterprise.

In the continually changing environment you will inevitably be refining tools and adding new ways of working to adapt to changing conditions.

We recommend building regular reviews of team performance into your operating rhythm and sharing your Team Canvas whenever a new member joins. This will ensure that everyone is literally on the same page.

# Before we move on

The most adaptable people and teams almost always have a repeatable cycle of alignment, collaboration and learning, which enables them to navigate flexibly through changeable conditions to achieve great outcomes.

This loop-and-learn approach is much like you'd see among the crew of a racing yacht, and is characteristic of all enterprises where small, agile teams are key to success, such as military special forces, Olympic sports, first responders and performing arts.

In a fast-changing and uncertain environment, the ability to *spin the ACL* is mission critical. You're now ready to move on and deep dive into the next three chapters, in order to:

» align for total commitment

» collaborate as one

» make team learning a habit.

# Learnings

» The starting point for teamwork is a **shared understanding** of the purpose and characteristics of a top team.

» Three activities, **alignment**, **collaboration** and **learning** (ACL), are core to the DNA of high-performing teams.

» The ACL describes the natural **learning loop** of top teams and comprises:

  » **Align.** Commit to a shared direction and focus.

  » **Collaborate**. Share in the spirit of working as one.

  » **Learn**. Be open, agile and adaptable.

» **Operating rhythm** is the pace and tempo of rituals, routines and actions by which teams align, collaborate and learn. There is no right or wrong rhythm, just the underlying principle of using loop and learn to navigate through a changing context.

» The **Team Canvas** unpacks the ACL into six building blocks that underpin a team development process comprising five phases: **Evaluate**, **Envision**, **Assemble**, **Implement** and **Adapt**.

» Start by completing the **evaluation exercise** on the Team Canvas and then work through the phases in a nonlinear way to suit your needs and the needs of your team and organisation.